Washington's Masonic Correspondence

As Found Among the Washington Papers in the Library of Congress

Compiled from the original records, under the direction of the Committee on Library of the Grand Lodge of Pennsylvania, with annotations.

By

Julius F. Sachse

Librarian, Masonic Temple, Philadelphia

Cover art by Strobridge & Gerlach lithographers.

First Printing: Philadelphia, 1915
Press of The New Era Printing Company
Lancaster, Pa.

Copyright ©2015 by Broken Column Press
BrokenColumnPress.com
ISBN: 978-0-9966341-8-2

From the Office of the Right Worshipful Grand Master of Free and Accepted Masons in Pennsylvania

The position of eminence, the great respect and the profound reverence in which the name of Washington is enshrined in the hearts of the American people, and particularly so, with the members of this Fraternity, and of all true lovers of liberty and freedom wheresoever dispersed, is the reason, if any be needed, why everything relating to this great man and worthy brother should be preserved for the future generations, to be used by them as a guide, in the cultivation of those cardinal virtues of Honor and Integrity, that should ever characterize the conduct of a good man and a good Mason.

The collection and reproduction of the letters of Brother Washington, together with the text of this book, have been prepared under my supervision, and its publication is heartily approved.

J. Henry Wiliams

Grand Master.

February 22, A.D. 1915—A.L. 5915.

Table of Contents

Introduction i

Foreword iii

The Masonic Correspondence of Washington.....................................1

Correspondence with Watson & Cassoul, Nantes, France, August, 1782...13

Correspondence with Alexandria Lodge, No. 39, Virginia, December, 1783. 22

Correspondence with Alexandria Lodge, No. 39, Virginia, June, 1784..28

Correspondence with King David's Lodge, No. 1, Rhode Island, August,1790. 31

Correspondence with St. John's Lodge, No. 2 at Newbern, N. C., April, 1791..38

Correspondence with Prince George's Lodge, No. 16, Georgetown, S. C., April, 1791...44

Correspondence with Grand Lodge of South Carolina, May, 1791. ..50

Correspondence with Grand Lodge of Georgia, May, 1791...............57

Correspondence with Grand Lodge of Pennsylvania, January 3, 1792..61

Correspondence with Grand Lodge of Massachusetts, December, 1792..72

Correspondence with Grand Lodge of Pennsylvania, December, 1796..78

Correspondence with Alexandria Lodge, No. 22, Virginia. 86

Correspondence With Grand Lodge of Massachusetts, March, 1797..93

Correspondence with Grand Lodge of Maryland, November, 1798..101

Correspondence with G. W. Snyder, 1798. 109

Introduction

George Washington's Masonic correspondence should be of interest to any American Freemason. His membership and involvement in the lodges is of paramount importance, given the amount of weight, respect, even deification he is given in U.S. Freemasonry.

In addition to his status as a general, a Revolutionary War hero, and an early American, Washington was highly revered as a Mason in his day, and was even offered the opportunity to be the Grand Master General over all the colonies at one point. This was more due to his standing as a well-known public figure than it was for his Masonic prowess, no doubt, but it still was a pivotal moment in early American Masonry.

Had the proposition extended by the Grand Lodge of Pennsylvania been adopted, we might today be holden under a Grand Lodge of the United States or some similar grand body, rather than the loosely connected system of state-based independent grand lodges we have today. Indeed, there were further movements to try to organize the grand lodges into an American grand lodge of one sort or the other, none of which was successful. Had the individual colonial grand lodges agreed to form a larger body, we would likely not been able to enjoy the same distinct flavors created by having come about separately. In this way, the failure to promote our dear Brother Washington was a blessing in the long run, although that surely could not have been known at the time.

The letters in this book show the concern our brother had for the fraternity and also show his commitment to it. What I find interesting is that, although he was surely a well-loved brother, and as much as he is loved today, the extent to which he corresponded on topics of Masonry with his brothers is pretty lackluster. For a brother so loved that his portrait could probably be found in almost every lodge in the country, he really had little contact with his own lodge, at least evidenced by this collection of letters.

Washington served as the charter Worshipful Master of Alexandria Lodge No. 22 when it received its charter from the Grand Lodge of Virginia, and was elected to serve a second year in that capacity, but lodge records do not indicate that he was a regular attendee. In fact, during his second year as Worshipful Master, he was inaugurated as President of the United States, and, no doubt, those duties were more important than the Masonic ones he had taken on.

Regardless of the level of his personal day-to-day involvement in and management of his lodge, George Washington is still clearly an important figure in American Freemasonry. It is my personal opinion that the emphasis placed on this one singular figure is overkill. We need to remember that Washington was a man whose greatness came from a series of circumstances, rather than solely from his personal values and makeup. Such is the nature of greatness. Many of us could potentially become labeled as heroes of our nations if put in the right circumstances. Was Washington a great man? History says yes and I concur. Was he, by nature, greater than another man, given the same opportunities and situations? I have my doubts. I may be labeled as a Masonic heretic for saying such a thing, but I believe that this viewpoint reinforces the nature of the level on which we travel, and more than bring down a good man such as Bro. Washington, it gives us all hope of being capable of greatness, and thus his equal.

Carl E. Weaver
Arlington, Virginia
October 2015

Foreword

Washington's Masonic correspondence as found among the Washington papers in the Manuscript department of the Library of Congress, affords an insight of the great esteem in which Washington held the Masonic Fraternity, of which since his early days he had been an honored member.

This is further shown by his great courtesy to the Brethren, in his replies to their addresses, no matter whether they were from a Grand or Subordinate Lodge. In this collection, were also found some of the original drafts of Washington's replies, together with copies of the various masonic addresses and letters to him, and in the case of Dominie Snyder, press copies of his answers.

In the present work an attempt has been made to group this matter together in chronological order, also to show some of the surroundings and conditions under which this correspondence was made, and of the Brethren who were prominent in the presentation of these Eleven Addresses, which came to him from Seven of the Thirteen Colonies.

A complete set of photostatic facsimiles of these documents in the Library of Congress, has been secured for the Museum of the Grand Lodge of Pennsylvania. Efforts were also made to obtain photographic copies of such of the Washington Masonic letters as were still in existence, which were successful except in two instances as noted in the text.

It will be noted that on April 30, 1789, Washington, while Master of his Lodge, was inaugurated President of the United States; this is the only instance where one of the fourteen Presidents, who were Members of our Fraternity was a Master of a Lodge during their term as President.

The esteem in which Washington held the Masonic Fraternity, is shown by the fact, that in almost every case he had both the address and his reply, copied upon opposite pages of one of his folio letter-books, now in the Library of Congress. These copies are respectively in the handwriting of Washington's private secretaries, viz:—Major William Jackson: Tobias Lear: Bartholomew Dandridge and G. W. Craik.

In addition to the above copies we have Washington's original drafts of his letters to Watson and Cassoul, to the Grand Lodges of Massachusetts, South Carolina, and Maryland, to Paul Revere, and as before stated press copies of his answers to Mr. Snyder.

A perusal of these original documents, as here presented, affords an excellent illustration of the *entente cordiale*, which existed between Washington and his Masonic Brethren.

Upon the other hand, how the Masonic Fraternity, during Washington's lifetime, venerated their august Brother, is shown by the addresses of this correspondence as retained by Washington.

Also by the various Masonic Memorial services held, after Washington's death, the chief of which was in Philadelphia, under the auspices of the Grand Lodge of Pennsylvania. The Masonic services held in every State of the Union, the many Eulogies and Sermons delivered and printed are matters of history.

How this veneration of the great Washington continued during the past years, is shown by the fact that there are no less than 53 Masonic Lodges in the United States, named after the illustrious Brother. This is independent of the numerous Royal Arch Chapters, Commanderies, and other Masonic bodies, that bear the name "Washington."

Washington Lodges are found in thirty-eight of the forty-eight States of the American Union.

The other ten States, which thus far have no "Washington Lodge" within their Jurisdiction, are Mississippi and Texas, together with the newer western States lately admitted into the American Union, viz:—Nevada, North Dakota, Montana, Idaho, Wyoming, Utah, New Mexico and Arizona.

In addition to the fifty-three Washington Lodges, there is also one each in Canada, the Island of Cuba and the District of Columbia.

In the Masonic Fraternity throughout the world, the name of Washington is ever kept in remembrance, as one of the brightest luminaries in the Masonic constellation, one of the most prominent examples, being his full length oil portrait in Masonic clothing in the Hall of the Grand Lodge of England at London.

Acknowledgments are due to the Hon. Herbert Putnam, Librarian of Congress, for placing these documents at the disposal of the writer, and giving permission to have photostat copies made of same; also to J. Henry Williams, Esq., R. W. Grand Master of Masons in Pennsylvania and Masonic Jurisdiction thereunto belonging, for suggestions and encouragement in the preparation of this work.

Julius F. Sachse.

Philadelphia, February 22, A.D. 1915—A.L. 5915.

Julius F. Sachse

The Masonic Correspondence
of Washington

Much has been written pro and con about Washington
and his connection with the Masonic Fraternity. Thus far no
complete set of his Masonic writings have been compiled or
published. Such portions as have been printed were fragmentary,
and issued for what may be called local purposes.

How careful Washington was of his Masonic
correspondence is shown by the fact that he had copies made, in
his private letter books, of most all letters sent him by the various
Masonic Grand and Subordinate bodies, and his answers thereto,
usually upon opposite pages. He thus had both the addresses and
his reply at hand for easy reference. This fact shows the esteem in
which Washington held his Brethren of the Masonic Fraternity, as
well as his own opinion of Freemasonry.

These letter-books are now in the Library of Congress,
and photostat copies of such as relate to Freemasonry have been
made for the Library of the Grand Lodge of Pennsylvania.

As to the authenticity of the Washington Letter Books,
and how they came into the possession of the United States
Government is explained by the following statement by Mr.
Galliard Hunt, chief Manuscript division, Library of Congress:[1]

"They are a part of the Washington papers in
"the Government's possession, purchased from the
"Washington family, one lot in 1834 and the re-
"mainder in 1849, and deposited in the Department
"of State until 1903, when, by the President's order,
"they were sent to this Library. They range in date
"from 1754 to 1799. Some of them are partly
"or wholly in Washington's hand-writing, and others
"in the writing of his secretaries and their clerks.

1

"There are no volumes of press copies, but there are
"some press copies among the papers."

Washington in writing his answer to the various greetings,
in most cases would first make a rough copy of his reply, then
digest, alter, correct or change such parts or sentences as he
thought proper. Then after deliberate consideration, a fair copy
would be made either by Washington or one of his Secretaries and
signed by him, and sent to the Masonic bodies for which they
were intended.

Fortunately some of the original drafts of these Masonic
letters have come down to us; thus far five autographic copies
have been found among the Washington papers in the Library of
Congress at Washington.

1. Draft of letter written at Newburg, New York, August
19, 1782, to Watson and Cassoul of Nantes, France, thanking
them for the Masonic Apron, embroidered by the nuns at Nantes,
and which is now in possession of Alexandria-Washington Lodge,
No. 22, at Alexandria, Virginia.

2. To the Grand Lodge of Massachusetts.

3. To the Grand Lodge of Pennsylvania.

4. To the Grand Lodge of South Carolina.

5. To the Grand Lodge of Maryland; this draft is a two-
page letter written upon a letter sheet and shows many changes
and corrections; it is dated 1798.

In addition to the above original drafts there were found
several addresses and the accompanying answers, which thus far
have never been published, in fact no mention of them has ever
appeared in print, viz:—

1. An address from the Grand Lodge of Georgia, together with Washington's reply.

2. A letter to Paul Revere, Grand Master of Massachusetts and his Grand Officers.

3. An address from the Brethren of Prince George's Lodge, No. 16, Georgetown, South Carolina, presented to President Washington during his visit to South Carolina, April 30, 1791, also his reply to same.

4. An address from the Brethren of St. John's Lodge, No. 2, of Newbern, North Carolina, and the reply to same.

Photostat copies of the above have also been obtained which make the most complete collection of the Masonic Correspondence of Washington which has thus far been compiled.

A careful study of this correspondence so carefully cherished by Washington puts an entirely new phase upon Washington's connection with the Masonic Fraternity, and his esteem of Freemasonry.

These papers absolutely thrust aside all of the statements, arguments and libels, brought forth by our misguided enemies at the time of the Anti-Masonic craze during the last century, and in a small way kept alive even down to the present day by some people who are blinded by their ignorance or malice.

Referring to some of their published statements that Washington never belonged to the Masonic Fraternity, and that there were no authentic Masonic letters nor copies thereof among his records so frequently made during the political Anti-Masonic craze, which swept over New England and the Middle States about eighty-five years ago, the following quotations from the Masonic literature of the period will prove interesting examples.

One of the chief statements made by these people, and brought before all their conventions and heralded in the public prints was: "That though General Washington caused to be carefully copied in books kept for that purpose, all his letters on every subject, no trace whatever of any of the five letters under consideration,[2] nor any letters to any other Lodge or Masonic body whatever, are to be found among the records of his correspondence."[3]

The chief authority upon whom the leaders of the Anti-Masonic movement at that time depended in their defamation of Washington, was Jared Sparks of Boston, who at the time was engaged writing a life of Washington, and then had access to all the Washington letter-books and papers, and from his connection with the Washington correspondence, was supposed to be the best qualified to pass upon their authenticity.

Another of the charges made by the Anti-Masonic bigots whose chief object was to controvert facts was:

"That although Washington was *extremely scrupulous* in preserving his correspondence with all public or private bodies, there is not a line of his *relating to Freemasonry*, to be found among all his papers, except the correspondence with Mr. Snyder![4] It is also a fact, that Washington was equally scrupulous in dating his letters, and it is believed that not one can be found, which is without a date."[5]

It appears that the chairman of a committee of citizens of Boston called upon the officers of the Grand Lodge of Massachusetts to submit their two Washington letters to Jared Sparks for his inspection. This the Grand Officers refused to do.

In return Sparks sent the following letter to the Chairman:

"Boston, February 18, 1833.

"*Sir*,—I received this morning your letter of the 15th instant, in which you inquire:

"Whether I have yet seen or had in my possession any original letter or letters, in the hand writing of General Washington, addressed to any body of men denominating themselves Freemasons.

"In reply, I can only state that I have seen no letters from General Washington of the kind described in yours, nor received any communication on the subject, either verbal or written.[6]

"I am, Sir,
"Very respectfully,
"Your ob't servant,
"Jared Sparks."

How Sparks could have overlooked the numerous entries in the letter books whose numbers and folios are here quoted, also the drafts of replies in Washington's hand-writing and signed by him (copies of which are here given in this work), can only be accounted for by the fact that he must have been carried away by the political excitement of the day.

Washington's connection with the Masonic Fraternity has been exhaustively traced by Brother James M. Lamberton, Past Master of Perseverance Lodge, No. 21, in his address "Washington as a Freemason," from the day of his entrance into Fredericksburg Lodge, No. 4, of Virginia, September 1, 1752, until the day of his death, December 14, 1799, before the Grand Lodge of Pennsylvania, at its celebration of the Sesqui-Centennial Anniversary of the Initiation of Brother George Washington into the Fraternity of Freemasons,[7] held in the Masonic Temple, in the city of Philadelphia on Wednesday, November 5, 1902.

It must also be remembered that Washington made a public profession of his membership in Philadelphia, Monday, December 28, 1778, when he walked in procession with his brethren of the Grand Lodge of Pennsylvania, from the College at

Fourth and Arch Streets to Christ Church on Second Street above Market Street, Philadelphia, where, after a prayer by Rev. William White, a sermon was preached for the "[Benefit of the POOR] by appointment of and before | The General Communication | of | Free and Accepted | MASONS | of the | State of PENNSYLVANIA, | on Monday, December 28, 1788, | Celebrated, agreeable to their Constitution, | as the Anniversary of | ST. JOHN the Evangelist, | by William Smith, D.D., | Provost of the College and Academy of Philadelphia." |

This Sermon was printed and dedicated to Brother Washington and a copy sent to him, which was bound with other pamphlets in a volume lettered "Masonic Sermons," and is so mentioned in the inventory of his estate and now in the Boston Athenæum.[8] At this service over four hundred pounds were collected for the relief of the poor.

Rev. Brother William Smith, D.D., preached a number of Masonic Sermons in Pennsylvania, Delaware and Maryland; three of which delivered at the request of the Grand Lodge of Pennsylvania were printed, viz.:

Sermon 1.—On Brotherly Love, &c. Preached on the Anniversary of St. John the Baptist, June 24, 1755,

Sermon 2.—Preached on Monday, December 28, 1778, celebrated as the Anniversary of St. John the Evangelist. With an Appendix on the Character of Lucius Quintius Cincinnatus,

Sermon 3.—Preached before the Grand Lodge of Communication, on St. John the Baptist's day, June 24, 1795.

Original copies of the above are in the Library of the Grand Lodge of Pennsylvania.

Rev. Brother Smith reprinted the above in a Volume of Sermons with the following note:[9]

"N. B. The above three Sermons were preached at the request of the Grand Lodge of Communication, for Pennsylvania, and contains in substance all that the Author thinks it necessary to bequeath to the Brotherhood, by way of Sermons, preached at different times and in sundry of the neighboring States, during 48 Years past."

By referring to the following letters and Documents it is shown that Washington's interest in Freemasonry and the Fraternity continued until the time of his death.

These documents cover the period from 1782 to 1798.

As these copies in our possession are photostat facsimiles of the original documents in the Library of Congress, there can never be any question of correctness or of their authenticity.

The finding and collating of this material will settle for all time to come the question of Washington's connection with the Ancient Fraternity, and his opinion and esteem of Freemasonry.

The earliest record we have of any Masonic Body proposing a masonic address to General Washington, was the resolution offered in King David's Lodge, No. 1, at Newport, Rhode Island, during Washington's visit to Newport in March, 1781, while the French Army under Rochambeau was quartered there. Washington arrived in Newport on the sixth of March and remained there until the thirteenth, when he left for Providence by way of Bristol.

It was in anticipation of this visit that the Brethren of King David's Lodge, of which Brother Moses Michael Hays[10] was Worshipful Master, that a masonic greeting to General Washington was proposed. The following entry from the old Minute Book of the Lodge will explain why the project failed to materialize.

W. M. KING DAVID'S LODGE, No. 1, NEWPORT, R. I., 1780-1781.
GRAND MASTER OF MASONS IN MASSACHUSETTS, 1788-1793.

Extract from the Records of King David's Lodge.

"Regular Lodge night, held at the house of Mr. James Tew, Wednesday evening, the 7th February, 1781. 5781.

"A motion being made that as our worthy brother, his Excellency General Washington, was daily expected amongst us, a committee should be appointed to prepare an address in behalf of the Lodge, to present him. Voted, That the Right Worshipful Master (Moses Michael Hays) together with brothers Seixas, Peleg Clark, John Handy, and Robert Elliot, be a committee for that purpose, and that they present the same to this Lodge at their next meeting for their approbation."

"At a Lodge held by request of the Right Worshipful Master, Feb. 14th, 1781. 5781,

"The committee appointed to draught an address to our worthy brother, His Excellency General Washington, report, that on inquiry they find General Washington not to be a Grand Master of North America; as was supposed, nor even Master of any particular Lodge. They are, therefore, of opinion that this Lodge would not choose to address him as a private brother at the same time, think it would not be agreeable to our worthy brother to be addressed as such.

"Voted, That the report of the committee be received, and that the address be entirely laid aside for the present."[11]

Now as to the cause for this uncertainty how to address Brother Washington, it will be recalled that just at that time, the proposition sent out by the Grand Lodge of Pennsylvania nominating General Washington as Grand Master of all the

Colonies, was then before the various grand bodies, but did not find favor in New England, in fact the Grand Lodge of Massachusetts was the chief objector, and finally defeated the scheme to elect Washington the Grand Master General.[12]

The means of intercourse between the different Masonic Bodies at that early day were so limited and uncertain that it offers a clear explanation for the uncertainty under which the brethren of King David's Lodge, No. 1, at Newport labored at that time.

During the Anti-Masonic craze in the last century, the above minute was extensively used by the political leaders of the Anti-Masonic party to strengthen their claim that Washington had never presided over any Masonic Lodge.

Following is a complete list of the Washington Masonic Correspondence, thus far found among the Washington papers in the Library of Congress.

- Draft of Letter to Watson and Cassoul, Nantes, France, August 10, 1782.

- Letter to Alexandria Lodge, No. 39, Virginia, December 28, 1783.

- Address from King David's Lodge, No. 1, Rhode Island, August 17, 1790, and Washington's Reply.

- Address from St. John's Lodge, No. 2, Newbern, North Carolina, April 20, 1791, and his reply.

- Address from Prince George's Lodge (Moderns) Georgetown, South Carolina, April 30, 1791, and his reply.

- Draft of reply to Grand Lodge of South Carolina, May 5, 1791.

- Address from Grand Lodge of Georgia, May 14, 1791, and his reply.

- Address from Grand Lodge of Pennsylvania, March, 1792, and his reply.

- Address of the Grand Lodge of Massachusetts, December 27, 1792, and his reply.

- Address from Grand Lodge of Pennsylvania, December 27, 1796, and his reply.

- Address from Alexandria Lodge, No. 22, Virginia, April 4, 1797, and his reply.

- Letter to Paul Revere and Grand Officers, April 24, 1797.

- Draft of Letter to Grand Lodge of Massachusetts in reply to an address, April 1797.

- Draft of a reply to an address from the Grand Lodge of Maryland, November 8, 1798.

- Letter from G. W. Snyder to Washington, August 22, 1798.

- Washington's Reply to Snyder, September 25, 1798.

- Washington's Reply to Snyder's letter of October 17, 1798.

Footnotes:

[1] Letter to Julius F. Sachse from Manuscript Division, December 19, 1914—in Library of Grand Lodge of Pennsylvania.

[2] The letters referred to by the Anti-Masons were the one to King David's Lodge at Newport, two to the Grand Lodge of Massachusetts, and one to Charleston, S. C., and to the Grand Lodge of Pennsylvania. The above five Masonic Letters were all that were known to the Anti-Masons at that time.

[3] "Vindication | of | General Washington | from the stigma | of adherence to | Secret Societies | by | Joseph Ritner |

Governor of the Commonwealth of Pennsylvania, |
communicated | by | request of the House of Representatives, to
that body,| on the 8th of March, 1837."

This address during the Anti-Masonic period was regarded as an
important state paper.

[4] Letter press copies of the Snyder letters were retained by
Washington. Photostat copies of same are in the Archives of the
Grand Lodge of Pennsylvania.

[5] "Proceedings of the Third State Anti-masonic Convention, of
Massachusetts, Worcester, 1832," p. 27.

[6] Vindication of Washington before quoted, p. 13.

[7] The Ancient Minute Book and Ledger of Fredericksburg
Lodge, No. 4, in Virginia, of which we have a photostat, is still in
possession of the Lodge, showing that "George Washington was
entered November 4, 1752, and on November 6, paid for his
entrance £2. 3. 0, March 3, 1753, George Washington was passed
to Fellow-Craft; August 4, 1753, George Washington was raised
Master Mason."

[8] Catalogue of Washington Collection in Boston Athenæum,
Boston, 1897, p. 185.

[9] Cf. "Works of William Smith, D.D.," Philadelphia, 1803, Vol.
II, pp. 27-88, also "Life and Correspondence of Rev. William
Smith, D.D.," Philadelphia, 1880, Vol. II, p. 9. *Et seq.*

[10] For an exhaustive sketch of Brother Moses Michael Hays, see
The American Freemason, Vol. V, p. 576.

[11] "Newport, ss. Newport, August 18th, A.D. 1832. I certify that
the extracts taken from the records of King David's Lodge,
Newport, contained in the above and three foregoing pages, have
been by me compared with the minutes contained in two books
purporting and appearing to be the original records of said Lodge,
and found to be true and accurate copies of the same.

"Quid attestor, "Geo. C. Mason.
"Jus. Peace and Pub. Not'y."

Cf. "Anti-masonic Republican Convention of Massachusetts held at Worcester, September 5-6, 1832," p. 23.

[12] For a full account of this episode, see "Freemasonry in Pennsylvania," Barratt and Sachse, Philadelphia, 1908, Vol. 1, Chapter XII; "Washington as General Grand Master," p. 393 *et seq.*

Correspondence with Watson & Cassoul, Nantes, France, August, 1782.

The earliest letter of General George Washington of Masonic Import known is the one written while in camp at Newburgh in New York, dated State of New York, August 10, 1782, to the firm of Watson and Cassoul in Nantes, France, in which his friend, Brother Elkanah Watson was the chief partner, thanking the firm for the Masonic Apron and ornaments sent him from Nantes, France.

This apron is now in the possession of the Alexandria-Washington Lodge, No. 22, at Alexandria, Virginia.

Elkanah Watson in his Memoirs states:[13]

"Wishing to pay some mark of respect to our beloved Washington, I employed, in conjunction with my friend M. Cossoul, nuns in one of the conventsat Nantes to prepare some elegant Masonic ornaments, and gave them a plan for combining the American and French Flags on the apron designed for this use. They were executed in a superior and expensive style. We transmitted them to America, accompanied by an appropriate address."

By the above extract is shown beyond all doubt the error in the statement so repeatedly made, that the apron at Alexandria is the one made by the Marquise de Lafayette, and presented to Washington by General Lafayette, during his visit to Mount Vernon in 1784, and the one in the Museum of the Grand Lodge of Pennsylvania, that of Watson and Cassoul.[14]

Following letter was sent to Washington, together with the Masonic Apron and "Ornaments," by Messrs. Watson and Cassoul, from France under date "east of Nantes," 23d 1st Month, 5782.[15]

"To his Excellency, General Washington, America.

"*Most Illustrious and Respected Brother:*

"In the moment when all Europe admire and feel the effects of your glorious efforts in support of American liberty, we hasten to offer for your acceptance a small pledge of our homage. Zealous lovers of liberty and its institutions, we have experienced the most refined joy in seeing our chief and brother stand forth in its defence, and in defence of a newborn nation of Republicans.

"Your glorious career will not be confined to the protection of American liberty, but its ultimate effect will extend to the whole human family, since Providence has evidently selected you as an instrument in his hands, to fulfill his eternal decrees.

"It is to you, therefore, the glorious orb of America, we presume to offer Masonic ornaments, as an emblem of your virtues. May the Grand Architect of the Universe be the Guardian of your precious days, for the glory of the Western Hemisphere and the entire universe. Such are the vows of those who have the favor to be by all the known numbers."

"Your affectionate brothers,
"Watson & Cassoul."

"East of Nantes, 23ᵈ 1st Month, 5782."

Owing to the uncertain intercourse between the two countries, it was almost seven months before Brother Washington received the Masonic apron, ornaments and letter from France. He at that time was in camp with the army at Newburg on the Hudson.[16]

In reply Washington sent the following autograph letter to the donors in Nantes, viz.:

14

"State of New York

"Augt 10th 1782.

"Gent$^n.$

"The Masonick Ornam^{ts}
"which accompanied your Bro-
"therly Address of the 23^d of
"Jany last, tho' elegant in
"themselves, were rendered
"more valuable by the flattering
"sentiments, and affectionate
"manner, in which they were
"presented.—

"If my endeavours to
"avert the evil, with which this
"Country was threatned by a
"deliberate plan of Tyranny,
"should be crowned with the suc
"cess that is wished—The praise
"is due to the *Grand Architect*
"of the Universe; who did not see
"fit to suffer his superstructures
"and justice, to be subjected to the
"Ambition of the Princes of this
"World, or to the rod of oppression,
"in the hands of any power upon
"Earth.—

"For your affectionate
"Vows, permit me to be grateful;
"—and offer mine for true Brothers
"in all parts of the world; and

"to assure you of the sincerity
"with which I am

    Y[rs]

    "Mess[rs]
"Watson & Cosson[17]
"East of Nantes"

    This autograph letter from Washington to Messrs. Watson and Cassoul is now in the possession of the Grand Lodge of New York, who purchased it from a member of the Watson family in the year 1866 or 1867 at a cost of approximately $1,000, and is now framed and secured between two sheets of glass in the collection of the Committee of Antiquities of the Grand Lodge F. & A. M. of New York.[18]

    It is written upon two pages of an ordinary letter sheet, and was a copy of one written by Washington, with which he was not entirely satisfied, as shown by the changes made in the text before it was sent to France. The first copy Washington retained, and is now in the Library of Congress, and is here given for comparison, viz:

State of New York.
Aug.t 10.th 1782.

Gen.tr

The Masonick Orna:
ments which accompanied your
Brotherly address of the 23.d
of the first Month, tho' elegant
in themselves, were rendered
more valuable by the flattering
sentiments, and affectionate
manner, in which they were
offered. ———

If my endeavours to
avert the evil, with which
this Country was threatned, by
a deliberate plan of Tyranny,
should be crowned with the
success that is wished — the
praise is due to the <u>Grand</u>
<u>architect</u>

*Facsimile of the Original Draft of Washington's Letter to Watson and
Cassoul, New York, August 10, 1782.*

"State of New York,
"Augt 10th 1782.

"*Gent^n.*,

"The Masonick Orna-
"ments which accompanied your
"Brotherly Address of the 23d.
"of the first month, tho' elegant
"in themselves, were rendered
"more valuable by the flattering
"sentiments, and affectionate
"manner, in which they were
"offered.—

"If my endeavours to
"avert the evil, with which
"this Country was threatned, by
"a deliberate plan of Tyranny,
"should be crowned with the
"success that is wished—the
"praise is due to the *Grand*
"*Architect* of the Universe; who
see fit to
"who did not ^ suffer his superstruc
"tures & justice, to be subjected
ambition of the Princes of this world—or
"to the ^ rod of oppression, in the
"hands of any power upon Earth.

"For your affectionate
"vows, permit me to be grateful;
"and offer mine for true Brothers
"in all parts of the world; and

"to assure you of the sincerity

"with which I am,

Y^{rs}.

Endorsed

to

"Messrs. Watson &

"Cosson—Nantes

"10th Augt 1782."

A photographic facsimile of the letter now in New York, and a photostat of the original copy retained by Washington are in the collection of the Grand Lodge of Pennsylvania.

The firm of Watson and Cassoul of Nantes, France, acted as confidential agents of the American Government during the Revolutionary period, as is shown by their correspondence with Benjamin Franklin in the Franklin Mss. collection of the American Philosophical Society.[19] Elkanah Watson was also a bearer of despatches to Dr. Franklin.

Footnotes:

[13] "Men and Times of the Revolution, or Memoirs of Elkanah Watson," New York, 1856, pp. 135, 136.

[14] Cf. "Proceedings Grand Lodge of New York," 1867, p. 28.

[15] "Memoirs of Elkanah Watson," p. 135.

[16] Cf. "Itinerary of General Washington from June 15, 1775, to December 23, 1783," by William S. Baker, Philadelphia, 1892, p. 271.

[17] It will be noted that on both the draft and letter, Washington spells the name Cassoul—"Cosson."

[18] Catalogue of Antiquities and Curios, Grand Lodge F. & A. M., New York, Class J, No. 1, New York, 1905.

[19] Cf. "Calendar of the Papers of Benjamin Franklin in the Library of the American Philosophical Society," edited by I. Minis Hays, Volume V, p. 312.

Correspondence with Alexandria Lodge, No. 39, Virginia, December, 1783.

The next Masonic Letter of Brother Washington of which we have any knowledge is the one written in answer to a letter sent him, upon his return to civil life by the Brethren of Lodge No. 39, on the register of the Grand Lodge of Pennsylvania, which met at Alexandria, Virginia.

December 23, 1783, General Washington presented himself to "The United States in Congress Assembled," at Annapolis, Maryland, and resigned his Commission that he had received on June 17, 1775, as Commander-in-Chief of the Armies of the United States.

Upon Christmas Eve he returned to Mount Vernon, whereupon the Brethren at Alexandria, who, it must be remembered, were working under a Pennsylvania Warrant, at once sent the following Address signed by the Officers of Lodge No. 39, to Brother Washington at Mount Vernon,[20] viz.:

"*Sir.* Whilst all denominations of people bless the happy occasion of your excellency's return to enjoy private and domestic felicity, permit us, sir, the members of Lodge No. 39, lately established in Alexandria, to assure your excellency, that we, as a mystical body, rejoice in having a brother so near us, whose preeminent benevolence has secured the happiness of millions; and that we shall esteem ourselves highly honored at all times your excellency shall be pleased to join us in the needful business."

"We have the honor to be, in the name and behalf of No. 39, your excellency's

"Devoted friends and brothers,

"Robert Adam, M.
"E. C. Dick, S. W.

"J. Allison, J. W.
"Wm. Ramsay, *Treas.*"

"His Excellency General Washington."

Two days later Brother Washington sent following reply,[21] viz.:

"Mount Vernon 28th Decr. 1783.

"*Gentlemen*:

"With pleasing sensibility
"I received your favor of the 26th, and
"beg leave to offer you my sincere thanks
"for the favorable sentiments with
"which it abounds.—

"I shall always feel pleasure
"when it may be in my power to ren-
"der service to Lodge N° 39, and in
"every act of brotherly kindness to the
"Members of it; being with great truth.

"Your affecte Brother
"and Obedt Servant

"Rob[t] Adam Esq[r] Master,
"& the Wardens & Treas[r]
"of Lodge N° 39."

No copy of either address nor reply of this correspondence has thus far been found among the Washington papers in the Library of Congress, by the present writer.

Brother Robert Adam, the Master of Alexandria Lodge, No. 39, was a Son of the Rev. John Adam, D.D., and Janet Campbell, of Kelbride, Scotland, was born May 4, 1731; he emigrated to America in 1753, and, after a short residence at Annapolis, Md., established himself at a pleasant country residence in Fairfax County, Virginia, about four miles from Alexandria. He was a gentleman of refined taste, cultivation and wealth, and interested himself in everything that could promote the prosperity of his adopted home.

Moun Verron 28th Dec.r 1783

Gentlemen

> *With a pleasure sensibility I received your favor of the 26th, and beg leave to offer you my sincere thanks for the favorable sentiments with which it abounds. —*
> *I shall always feel pleasure when it may be in my power to render service to Lodge N.o 39, and in every act of brotherly kindness to the members of it; being with great truth*
> *Your affect.e Brother and Obed.t Servant*
> *G.o Washington*

Rob.t Adam Esq.r Master,
& the Wardens & Treas.r
of Lodge N.o 39

Washington's Reply to Alexandria Lodge, No. 39. Original in Alexandria-Washington Lodge, No. 22, Alexandria, Virginia.

It appears that during his residence at Annapolis, he was made a Mason in a clandestine or irregular Lodge, and in the year

1783 applied for a dispensation from the Grand Master of Pennsylvania, to apply to Lodge No. 2, for initiation and membership.

Brother Dr. Elisha Cullen Dick, Senior Warden of Lodge No. 39, was a native of Pennsylvania, born near Marcus Hook, in Delaware County, about 1753, and died at Alexandria, Va., September 22, 1825. He was a son of Archibald Dick, a member of Lodge No. 2 at Philadelphia, and joined the same Lodge, September 15, 1779.[22] Brother Elisha C. Dick was a graduate of the old Pequea Academy, and of the College of Pennsylvania. He began the study of medicine under Drs. William Shippen and Benjamin Rush. After graduating he settled in Alexandria, Va., and at once became active in Masonic circles in that city, and was instrumental in having the petition presented to the Grand Lodge of Pennsylvania for a warrant, which was granted under the name and number "Alexandria Lodge No. 39."

Upon the records of the Lodge, Brother Dick appears as both predecessor and successor of Brother Washington as Master. Brother Dick was the first consulting physician in Washington's last illness, and also conducted the Masonic services at Washington's funeral on December 18, 1799. A biography of Dr. Dick is in the Library of the Grand Lodge of Pennsylvania.

Brother John Allison, the Junior Warden of Lodge No. 39, had served as Major in the 1st Virginia State Regiment, and later as Lieutenant Colonel.

Brother William Ramsay, Treasurer of Lodge No. 39, was an old personal friend of Washington.

For a history of Alexandria Lodge, No. 39, warranted by the Grand Lodge of Pennsylvania, February 3, 1783, which was constituted on the second floor of a large three-story frame building, known as the "Lamb Tavern," on the twenty-fifth of February, 1783, the Masonic student is referred to "Old Masonic

Lodges of Pennsylvania," Philadelphia, 1913, Chapter XLVI, pp. 153-168.

This tavern was situated on the west side of Union Street, between Prince and Duke Streets, Alexandria, the site of which is now known as No. 55 South Union Street.[23]

Footnotes:

[20] Cf. "Old Masonic Lodges of Pennsylvania—Moderns and Ancients," Julius F. Sachse, Philadelphia, 1913, Vol. II, p. 157. Also *Vide* "Washington the Man and the Mason," by Charles H. Callahan, published under the auspices of the "Memorial Temple Committee of the George Washington Masonic National Memorial Association," Washington, D. C., 1913.

[21] Original among Washington relics in Alexandria-Washington Lodge, No. 22, Alexandria, Virginia. Facsimile in Washington collection of Grand Lodge of Pennsylvania.

[22] Elisha C. Dick's petition was presented in Lodge No. 2, September 14, 1779, approved and entered by virtue of a dispensation from the Grand Master, September 15; passed and raised, September 23. "Freemasonry in Pennsylvania," Vol. I, pp. 352, 353.

[23] Cf. "The Lodge of Washington," by F. L. Brocket, Alexandria, Va., 1876.

Correspondence with Alexandria Lodge, No. 39, Virginia, June, 1784.

The next Washington letter of Masonic import in chronological order is his reply to an invitation to join the brethren of Alexandria Lodge, No. 39, in the celebration of St. John the Baptist's Day, June 24, 1784, to which Washington sent the following reply, accepting the fraternal invitation.

"Mount Vernon, June 19, 1784.[24]

"*Dear Sir.* With pleasure, I received the invitation of the master and members of Lodge No. 39, to dine with them on the approaching anniversary of St. John the Baptist. If nothing unforeseen at present interferes, I will have the honor of doing it. For the polite and flattering terms in which you have expressed their wishes, you will please accept my thanks."

"With esteem and respect,
"I am, dear sir,
"Your most Ob't serv't

"Wm. Herbert, Esquire."

No copy of this invitation nor acceptance, has thus far been found among the Washington papers.

The original of this letter is also said to be among the relics of Alexandria-Washington Lodge, No. 22. As no facsimile copy was obtainable, an engrossed copy for same was substituted in the collection of Grand Lodge of Pennsylvania.

This banquet was held at Wise's tavern[25] and was participated in by Washington, who upon this festive occasion was elected an honorary Member of Lodge No. 39, upon the Pennsylvania register, and thus became a Pennsylvania Freemason, and his name is duly recorded as such upon the minutes of Lodge No. 39.

This fact further contradicts the Anti-Masonic arguments based upon the Snyder letter so extensively used during the years 1826-1833, that Washington never belonged to any Masonic Lodge, after his initiation in the Fredericksburg Lodge in 1752.

The above note as recorded upon the Minutes of Alexandria Lodge, No. 39, shows that Washington was in complete harmony with the Masonic Fraternity; further, that by his acceptance of membership, Washington became a Pennsylvania Mason.

Among the cherished relics in the Alexandria Lodge, there is none more valuable than the Masonic portrait of Brother Washington, which forms the frontispiece of this volume. This was painted from life in pastel, by William Williams, at Philadelphia in 1794.

In the year 1910 a facsimile of this portrait was made in oil by Miss Fanny M. Burke, an artist of repute, and a great-granddaughter of Thomas Jefferson. This replica made for the Grand Lodge of Pennsylvania is the only one ever made of this portrait and shows Brother Washington as a man and Mason, neither heroized nor idealized.[26]

Footnotes:

[24] "Washington and his Masonic Compeers," by Sidney Hayden, New York, 1866, p. 104.

[25] John Wise's tavern, in which the above Masonic Banquet was held, is a large three-story brick building still standing on high ground at the northeast corner of Cameron and Fairfax Streets, Alexandria. At that time it had an unobstructed view of the Potomac.

[26] *Vide* "Abstract of Proceedings of the Proceedings Grand Lodge of Pennsylvania, During the Year 1910," pp. 110-117.

Correspondence with King David's Lodge, No. 1, Rhode Island, August,1790.

The next correspondence in chronological order is the letter, sent in reply to the Address delivered by the Brethren of King David's Lodge, No. 1, at Newport, Rhode Island, to President Washington, August 17, 1790, during his visit to New England.

By referring to the Minutes of this old Lodge following entry is found:

"At a Lodge, called by request of several Breth-
"ren on Tuesday evening, August 17, 5790, an
"Entered Apprentice Lodge being opened in due
"form proceeded to business, when it was proposed
"to address the President of the United States.
"The R. W. Master (Moses Seixas) Henry Sher-
"burne, and the Secretary, [William Littlefield]
"were appointed a committee for that purpose,
"after which the Lodge closed."[27]

Following address was prepared and according to local tradition was publicly presented, by the Committee to President Washington, in the Venerable Sanctuary of the Jewish Congregation at Newport; the Brethren of King David's Lodge being present:

"To George Washington, *President of the United States of America.*

"We the Master, Wardens, and Brethren of
"King David's Lodge in New Port Rhode Island
"with joyful hearts embrace this opportunity to
"greet you as a Brother, and to hail you welcome
"to Rhode Island. We exult in the thought that

"as Masonry has always been patronised by the
"wise, the good, and the great, so that it stood
"and ever will stand, as its fixtures are on the
"immutable pillars of faith, hope, and charity.

"With unspeakable pleasure we gratulate
"you as filling the presidential chair with the
"applause of a numerous and enlightened people
"Whilst at the same time we felicitate ourselves
"in the honor done the brotherhood by your many
"exemplary virtues and emanations of goodness
"proceeding from a heart worthy of possessing
"the ancient mysteries of our craft; being persuaded
"that the wisdom and grace with which heaven
"has endowed you, will square all your thoughts,
"words, and actions by the eternal laws of honor,
"equity, and truth, so as to promote the advancement
"of all good works, your own happiness, and that
"of mankind.

"Permit us then, illustrious Brother,
"cordially to salute you with three times three
"and to add our fervent supplications that the
"sovereign architect of the universe may always
"encompass you with his holy protection.

"Moses Seixas[28] *Master*
"New Port Augt 17, 1790. *Committee.*
"H^y Sherburne
"By order
"Wm Littlefield, *Sec^y.*"

Brother Moses Seixas was born in New York, March 28,
1744; died in New York City, November 29, 1809. He was a

merchant in Newport, Rhode Island, and one of the founders of the Newport Bank of Rhode Island, of which he was cashier until his death. He succeeded Brother Moses M. Hays as Worshipful Master of King David's Lodge at Newport. He was also the first Grand Master of the Grand Lodge of Rhode Island. It was Moses Seixas who addressed a letter of welcome in the name of the Jewish congregation to George Washington when the latter visited Newport, and it was to him that Washington's answer was addressed.

The Town Hall at Newport being out of repair at that time the ancient Jewish Synagogue on the main street was used, upon that and several other public occasions. It is an interesting fact that this sacred edifice is still preserved in the same condition as it was during the Colonial period.

So far as known this address was the first of Masonic import made to Washington as President. Unfortunately, the exact date of presentation and receipt of his answer is not known to a certainty, as there does not appear to be any date upon either the original documents or the copies in Washington's letter book.

The original address and Washington's reply to the Master, Wardens and Brethren of King David's Lodge in Newport, the latter signed in autograph by Washington, are in the Athenæum collection at Boston, Massachusetts.[29]

Following copy of the President's answer is taken from his letter book.[30] Both address and answer in the letter book are in the handwriting of Major William Jackson, secretary to the President.

A photostat of the original entry is in the Archives of the Grand Lodge of Pennsylvania. It will be noted that there is neither place nor date given.

29.

To the master, Wardens, and Brethren of
King Davids Lodge in Newport Rhode Island.

Gentlemen

I receive the welcome which you give me to Rhode-Island with pleasure, and I acknowledge my obligations for the flattering expressions of regard, contained in your address, with grateful sincerity.

Being persuaded that a just application of the principles, on which the masonic fraternity is founded, must be promotive of private virtue and public prosperity, I shall always be happy to advance the interests of the society, and to be considered by them as a deserving brother.

My best wishes, Gentlemen, are offered for your individual happiness.

G Washington

Facsimile of Reply to King David's Lodge, No. 1, Newport, R. I. Letter Book II, Folio 29.

34

President Washington arrived at Newport, R.I., at eight o'clock on Tuesday morning, August 17, 1790. On the next day, Wednesday, the President and his suite left on the Packet "Hancock" at nine o'clock in the morning for Providence.

His company consisted of Governor Clinton of New York, Thomas Jefferson, Secretary of State, Senator Theodore Foster, Judge Blair, Mr. Smith of South Carolina and Mr. Gorman of New Hampshire; members of Congress.[31]

Washington left Providence, Saturday, August 21, and arrived in New York upon the following day, Sunday, August 22, 1790,[32] and sent the following reply to the Newport Brethren:

"To the Master, Wardens, and Brethren of
"King Davids Lodge in Newport Rhode Island."

"*Gentlemen,*

"I receive the welcome which you
"give me to Rhode Island with pleasure, and I
"acknowledge my obligations for the flattering
"expressions of regard, contained in your address,
"with grateful sincerity.

"Being persuaded that a just
"application of the principles, on which the Masonic
"Fraternity is founded, must be promotive of
"private virtue and public prosperity, I shall
"always be happy to advance the interests of
"the Society, and to be considered by them as
"a deserving brother.

"My best wishes, Gentlemen,
"are offered for your individual happiness."[33]

> **BROTHER,**
>
> **Y**OU are defired to meet the MASTER and BRE-THREN of LODGE No. 39, Ancient YORK MA-SONS, at *their room*
>
> at **7** o'Clock this Evening. By Order of the Mafter,
>
> *D Ramfay* Secretary.
>
> Alexandria, *August 28*, 178 6

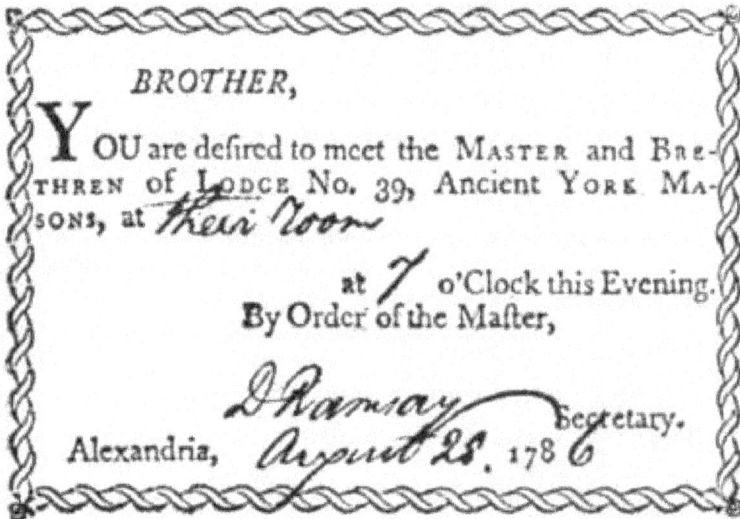

Facsimile of Notice sent to Brother Washington at Mount Vernon to Attend his Lodge. Treasured by the Wife of President Madison until her Death. Original in Archives of Grand Lodge of Pennsylvania. Mss. Vol. A, Folio 81.

Footnotes:

[27] A copy of the Extracts from the Records of King David's Lodge, No. 1, as made by Ara Hildreth, Esq., is in the Archives of the Grand Lodge of Pennsylvania, Mss. Volume Q, R.I. 7.

Cf. also a verified copy of the Minute in "Proceedings of the Anti-Masonic Republican Convention of Massachusetts, Boston, 1832," p. 22.

[28] *Vide* "The Jews and Masonry in the United States," by Samuel Oppenheim, New York, 1810, p. 22 *et seq.*

[29] Cf. "Catalogue of the Washington Collection in the Boston Athenæum," Boston, 1897, p. 331.

[30] Letterbook II, p. 29.

[31] Cf. "Washington after the Revolution," W. S. Baker, Philadelphia, 1898, p. 192.

[32] Cf. *Pennsylvania Packet*, August 30-31 1790.

[33] Copy of Address in Letter Book II, pp. 27-28, Photostat of same in Archives of Grand Lodge of Pennsylvania.

Correspondence with St. John's Lodge, No. 2 at Newbern, N. C., April, 1791.

The next Masonic letter of President Washington was written, in answer to an address by the brethren of St. John's Lodge, No. 2, at Newbern, North Carolina, during his southern tour in 1791.

April 7, 1791, Washington started on a tour through the Southern States, by way of Fredericksburg, Richmond, and Petersburg, Virginia; Halifax, Tarborough, Newbern, and Wilmington, North Carolina; Georgetown, and Charleston, South Carolina; and Savannah, Georgia.

When advice of this proposed presidential visit reached Newbern, the brethren of St. John's Lodge, No. 2,[34] at the stated meeting held on April 1, 1791, passed the following resolution. "*Resolved*, that an address shall be presented to Brother George Washington, in behalf of this Lodge, on his arriving in this town."[35]

Upon his arrival at Newbern, N. C., April 20, following address was presented to the President,[36] which, together with the reply, has thus far never been in print or noted:

"To the President of the United States of America.

"The Address of St Johns Lodge No. 2 of Newbern.

"*Right Worshipful Sir,*

"We the Master, Officers, and Members of St. "Johns Lodge No 2, of Newbern, beg leave to hail "you welcome with three times three.

"We approach you not with the language of "adulation, but sincere fraternal affection—your

"works having proved you to be the true and faith-
"ful brother, the skilful and expert Craftsman, the
"just and upright man,   But the powers of elo-
"quence are too feeble to express with sufficient
"energy the cordial warmth with which our bosoms
"glow toward you.

"We therefore most ardently wish, most fervently
"and devoutly pray, That the Providence of the
"most high may strengthen, establish, and protect
"you, in your walk through this life; and when you
"shall be called off from your terrestrial labours by
"command of our divine grand master, and your
"operations sealed with the mark of his approbation,
"may your soul be eternally refreshed with the
"streams of living water which flow at the right
"hand of God, and when the supreme architect of
"all worlds shall collect his most precious jewels as
"ornaments of the celestial Jerusalem, may you
"everlastingly shine among those of the brightest
"lustre.

"We are in our own behalf, and that of the
"Members of this Lodge,

        "Right worshipful Sir;
"St Johns Lodge No. 2.
"Your true and faithful brethren
"April 20th 5791.
"Isaac Guion *Master.*
"Samuel Chapman *Senior Warden.*
"William Johnston, *Junior Warden.*
"Solomon Halling, Edw. Pasteur, Jas Carney, F. Lowthrop.
"*Members of the Committee.*"

To the President of the United States of America

The Address of St Johns. Lodge No 2. of Newbern

Right worshipful Sir.

We the Master. Officers. and members of St Johns Lodge No 2. of Newbern, beg leave to hail you welcome with three times three.

We approach you not with the language of adulation, but sincere fraternal affection. your works having proved you to be the true and faithful brother — the skilful and expert Craftsman. the just and upright man. — But the powers of eloquence are too feeble to express with sufficient energy the cordial warmth with which our bosoms glow towards you

We therefore most ardently wish — most fervently and devoutly pray — That the Providence of the most high may strengthen, establish, and protect you, in your walk through this life; and when you shall be called off

Facsimile of Address from St. John's Lodge, No. 2, Newbern, N. C. Letter Book II, Folio 47-48.

Brothers: Isaac Guion, Worshipful Master, Samuel Chapman, Senior Warden, William Johnston, Junior Warden, and Solomon Halling, signers to above petition had all seen service in the Continental Army during the Revolutionary War. Brother Guion served as Surgeon and Paymaster; Brother Chapman, Captain in 8th North Carolina, serving until the close of the War;

Brother Johnston, Captain in North Carolina Militia and present at Kings Mountain.

Brother Hailing was Surgeon of the 4th Carolina Regiment and served until the close of the War.

Washington's Reply[37] to the Brethren of St. John's Lodge.

"To the Master, Wardens, and Members of St John's Lodge No. 2 of Newbern.

"*Gentlemen,*

"I receive the cordial welcome which you
"are pleased to give me with sincere gratitude.

"My best ambition having ever aimed at
"the unbiassed approbation of my fellow-citizens,
"it is peculiarly pleasing to find my conduct
"so affectionately approved by a fraternity whose as-
"sociation is founded in justice and benevolence.

"In reciprocating the wishes contained
"in your address, be persuaded that I offer a sincere
"prayer for your present and future happiness.

"At the following Meeting of St. John's Lodge, No. 2, April 29, 1791, the Master laid before the Lodge the answer of Brother George Washington ordered that it be read, which being done, Resolved that it be entered on Minutes of this Lodge."[38]

"The Address to Brother Washington and his answer are both on the Minutes of the Lodge. The original letter may have been lost during the late unpleasantness, as the Lodge lost nearly everything it possessed."[39]

Footnotes:

[34] In the latter part of the eighteenth century, St. John's Lodge, No. 2, at Newbern, was very active, at which time it built a two-story theatre and Masonic Hall, and took part in a number of local matters.

[35] Extract from Minutes by Brother J. F. Rhem, M.D., Newbern, N. C.

[36] Letter Book 2, pp. 47-48 in Library of Congress, Washington, D. C.; photostat in Archives of Grand Lodge of Pennsylvania.

[37] *Ibid.*, p. 49; photostat in Archives of Grand Lodge of Pennsylvania.

[38] Extract from Minutes by Brother J. F. Rhem, M.D., Newbern, N. C.

[39] Brother J. F. Rhem, Newbern, N. C., in letter to Brother A. B. Andrews, Jr., December 14, 1914.

Correspondence with Prince George's Lodge, No. 16, Georgetown, S. C., April, 1791.

Washington left Newbern, North Carolina, under an escort of horse, April 22, 1791, and arrived at Georgetown, South Carolina, by way of Wilmington, N. C., Saturday, April 30, where he was received with a salute of cannon, and by a company of infantry, and during the afternoon was presented with the following address, by a Committee of Prince George's Lodge, No. 16 (Moderns), of Georgetown, South Carolina.

This Lodge was one of the original six Lodges, which had been warranted prior to 1756 in South Carolina, under the Jurisdiction of the Provincial Grand Lodge, and through it, the Grand Lodge of England. It is the only instance where a Lodge of the "Moderns" addressed Brother Washington:

"To Our illustrious Brother George Washington.

"*President of the United States.*

"At a time when all men are emulous to approach
"you to express the lively sensations you inspire as
"the Father of our country. Permit us the Brethren
"of Prince George's Lodge No. 16 to have our share
"in the general happiness in welcoming you to
"Georgetown, and the pleasure of reflecting that we
"behold in you the liberator of our country. the
"distributor of its equal laws, and a Brother of our
"most ancient and most honorable Order.

"At the same time indulge us in congratulating
"you on the truly honorable and happy situation in
"which you now stand, as the Grand Conductor of
"the political interests of these United States.

"Having by your manly efforts caused the beau-

"teous light of liberty to beam on this western hemi-
"sphere, and by the wisdom Heaven has graciously
"endowed you with established the liberties of
"America on the justest and firmest basis that was
"ever yet recorded in the annuals of history, you
"now enjoy the supremest of all earthly happiness
"that of diffusing peace, liberty, and safety to mil-
"lions of your fellow-citizens.

"As a true reward for your patriotic, noble and
"exalted services we fervently pray the Grand Archi-
"tect of the universe long to bless you with health,
"stability, and power to continue you the Grand
"Pillar of the arch of liberty in this vast empire,
"which you have been so eminently distinguished in
"raising to this pitch of perfection at which we now
"behold it.

"May the residue of your life be spent in ease
"content and happiness, and as the Great Parent of
"these United States may you long live to see your
"children flourish under your happy auspices and
"may you be finally rewarded with eternal happiness.

"We conclude our present address with a fervent
"wish that you will continue as you have hitherto
"been, the friend of our ancient and honorable
"Order, and of all worthy Masons.

    I. White
R. Grant *Committee from*
A^B. Cohen *Prince George's Lodge.*
Jos. Blyth.
J. Carson.

"George Town 30th April 1791."

Of the above signers, three of the brethren had served in the War for Independence, viz.: Brother Isaac White, Lieutenant in North Carolina Militia at Kings Mountain; Brother Reuben Grant, Ensign in the 6th North Carolina Infantry, and Brother Joseph Blythe, Surgeon in 1st North Carolina Regiment, taken prisoner at Charleston, May 12th, 1780; exchanged June 14, 1781; in 4th North Carolina in February, 1782, and served to close of war.

To our illustrious Brother George Washington
President of the United States

At a time when all men are emulous to approach you to express the lively sensations you inspire as the Father of our country – Permit us the Brethren of Prince George's lodge No 16 to have our share in the general happiness in welcoming you to Georgetown, and the pleasure of reflecting that we behold in you the Liberator of our country. The distributor of its equal laws, and a Brother of our most ancient and most honorable Order

At the same time indulge us in congratulating you on the truly honorable and happy situation in which you now stand, as the grand Conductor of the political interests of these United States

Having by your manly efforts caused the beauteous light of liberty to beam on this western Hemisphere, and by the wisdom Heaven has graciously endowed you with established the liberties of America on the justest and firmest bases that was ever yet recorded in the annals of history – you now enjoy the supremest of all earthly happiness that of diffusing peace, liberty and safety, to millions of your fellow-citizens.

As a due reward for your patriotic, noble, and exalted

[Handwritten text:]

services we fervently pray the grand Architect of the universe long to bless you with health, stability, and power to continue you the Grand Pillar of of the arch of liberty in this vast empire, which you have been so eminently distinguished in raising to this pitch of perfection at which we now behold it.

May the residue of your life be spent in ease content and happiness — and as the Great Parent of these United States may you long live to see your children flourish under your happy auspices and may you be finally rewarded with eternal happiness.

We conclude our present address with a fervent wish that you will continue as you have hitherto been, the friend of our ancient and honorable Order — and of all worthy masons

J. White
R. Grant
A. Cohen
Jno. Blyth
J. Carson

} Committee from Prince George's Lodge

George Town 30th April 1791.

Facsimile of Address from the Brethren of Prince George's Lodge, Folio No. 16, Georgetown, South Carolina, April, 1791. Letter Book II, 59-60.

The following reply unfortunately bears no date. Both address and reply were entered in Washington Letter Book, No. II, folio 60-61. It is not known what has became of the originals. No notice or copies of either of the above documents have thus far been published.

Washington's Reply.

"To the Brethren of Prince George's Lodge, No. 16.

"*Gentlemen*:

"The cordial welcome which you give me
"to George Town, and the congratulations, you are
"pleased to offer on my election to the chief
"magistracy receive my grateful thanks.

"I am much obliged by your good wishes
"and reciprocate them with sincerity, assuring the
"fraternity of my esteem, I request them to believe
"that I shall always be ambitious of being considered
"a deserving Brother.

Correspondence with Grand Lodge of South Carolina, May, 1791.

President Washington left Georgetown at six o'clock in the evening, May 1, 1791, reaching Charleston, South Carolina, Monday, May 2, in a twelve-oared barge rowed by twelve American captains of ships accompanied by a great number of boats with gentlemen and ladies in them, and two boats with music.[40] Brother Washington remained in Charleston until May 9.

Wednesday, May 4, 1791, General Mordecai Gist, an old companion in arms of Washington, and formerly Master of the Military Lodge in the Maryland line (No. 27 upon the register of Pennsylvania),[41] but now Grand Master of the Grand Lodge of Ancient York Masons of South Carolina, attended by the other present and past grand officers,[42] waited on their beloved brother, the president of the United States, and presented the following address:[43]

"*Sir*—Induced by a respect for your public and private character, as well as the relation in which you stand with the brethren of this society, we the Grand Lodge of the State of South Carolina, Ancient York Masons, beg leave to offer our sincere congratulations on your arrival in this state.

"We felicitate you on the establishment and exercise of a permanent government, whose foundation was laid under your auspices by military achievements, upon which have been progressively reared the pillars of the free republic over which you preside, supported by wisdom, strength, and beauty unrivalled among the nations of the world.

"The fabric thus raised and committed to your superintendence, we earnestly wish may continue to produce order and harmony to succeeding ages, and be the asylum of virtue to the oppressed of all parts of the universe.

"When we contemplate the distresses of war, the instances of humanity displayed by the Craft afford some relief to the feeling mind; and it gives us the most pleasing sensation to recollect, that amidst the difficulties attendant on your late military stations, you still associated with, and patronized the Ancient Fraternity.

"Distinguished always by your virtues, more than the exalted stations in which you have moved, we exult in the opportunity you now give us of hailing you brother of our Order, and trust from your knowledge of our institution, to merit your countenance and support.

"With fervent zeal for your happiness, we pray that a life so dear to the bosom of this society, and to society in general, may be long, very long preserved; and when you leave the temporal symbolic lodges of this world, may you be received into the celestial lodge of light and perfection, where the Grand Master Architect of the Universe presides.

"Done in behalf of the Grand Lodge.

"M. Gist, G. M."[44]

"Charleston, 2d May, 1791."

To this address Washington returned the following reply.[45]

"*Gentlemen*:—I am much obliged by the respect which you are so good as to declare for my public and private character. I recognize with pleasure my relation to the brethren of your Society, and I accept with gratitude your congratulations on my arrival in South Carolina.

"Your sentiments, on the establishment and exercise of our equal government, are worthy of an association, whose principles lead to purity of morals, and are beneficial of action.

"The fabric of our freedom is placed on the enduring basis of public virtue, and will, I fondly hope, long continue to protect the prosperity of the architects who raised it. I shall be happy, on every occasion, to evince my regard for the Fraternity. For your prosperity individually, I offer my best wishes."

This letter was probably destroyed with other Grand Lodge property when Columbia, South Carolina, was burned by Sherman's Army during the war between the States.[46]

Fortunately, the original draft of Washington's reply, was found among the Washington papers now in the Library of Congress. This is written upon two pages of a letter sheet: the first page shows a paragraph which was suppressed and did not appear upon the clear copy sent to the Grand Lodge of Ancient York Masons of South Carolina.

A photostat of this draft is in the collection of the Grand Lodge of Pennsylvania, viz.:

"To the Grand Lodge of the State of South "Carolina Ancient York Masons.

"*Gentlemen,*

"I am much obliged by the respect "which you are so good as to declare for my "public and private character. I recognise

"with pleasure my relation to the Brethren
"of your Society—and I accept with gratitude
"your congratulations on my arrival in
"South Carolina.

"*Your felicitations It is peculiarly*
general
"*pleasing to observe the ^ satisfaction expressed*
"*on the establishment and exercise of the*
"*federal government—*
"Your sentiments on the establishment
"and exercise of our equal government are
"worthy of an association, whose principles
"lead to purity of morals, and beneficence
"of action—The fabric of our freedom
"is placed on the enduring basis of
"public virtue, and will long continue
"to protect the Posterity of the architects
"who raised it.

"I shall be happy on every
regard
"occasion to evince my respect for the
"Fraternity, for whose happiness individually
"I offer my best wishes.

To the Grand Lodge of the State of South-Carolina
ancient york Masons.

Gentlemen

I am much obliged by the esteem
which you are so good as to declare for my
public and private character — I recognize
with pleasure my relation to the Brethren
of your society — and I accept with gratitude
your congratulations on my arrival in
South Carolina.

Your sentiments on the establishment
and exercise of our equal government are
worthy of an association, whose principles
lead to purity of morals, and beneficence

Facsimile of Draft of Washington's Reply to Address from Grand Lodge of
South Carolina, May, 1791.
Handwriting of Mayor William Jackson.

Upon the first page the four lines commencing with "Your felicitations" and ending with "federal government" were crossed out, and as above stated, were not in the reply sent to R. W. Grand Master Gist and his officers.

In the third line from the bottom the word "regard" is substituted for "respect."

Brother Gist was the original Warrant Master of the Regimental Lodge in the Maryland line, No. 27, on the Roster of the Grand Lodge of Pennsylvania. After the war, Brother Gist settled in Charleston, South Carolina, retaining his old Military

Warrant, and, in 1786, applied to the Grand Lodge of Pennsylvania, to renew this warrant, for a Lodge to be located at Charleston under the same number. This request was granted, and Brother Gist was again named as Warrant Master.

At the formation of the Grand Lodge of South Carolina Ancient York Masons in 1787, Brother Gist was elected Deputy Grand Master and served as such during the years 1787-88-89, and as Grand Master, 1790-1791.

Footnotes:

[40] Washington's Diary.

[41] Cf. "Old Masonic Lodges in Pennsylvania," Philadelphia, 1913, Vol. 2, p. 53 *et seq.*

[42] Brother William Drayton, Past Grand Master; Brother Mordecai Gist, Grand Master; Brother Thomas B. Bowen, Deputy Grand Master; Brother George Miller, Senior Grand Warden; Brother John Mitchell, Junior Grand Warden; Brother Thomas Gates, Grand Chaplain; Brother Robert Knox, Grand Treasurer; Brother Alexandrer Alexander, Grand Secretary; Brother Israel Meyers, Grand Tiler.

[43] *City Gazette*, Friday, May 6, 1791, p. 2, column 4.

[44] For full account of Lodge 27 and Brother Gist, *vide* "Old Masonic Lodges of Pennsylvania," before quoted, Vol. II, pp. 53-63.

[45] Cf. Hayden, "Washington and his Masonic Compeers," p. 135.

[46] William C. Mazyck, Right Worshipful Grand Secretary, G. L. of South Carolina.

Correspondence with Grand Lodge of Georgia, May, 1791.

On the way from Charleston, South Carolina, to Savannah, Georgia, Washington called on Mrs. Greene, the widow of late Brother General Nathaniel Greene, at her plantation called Mulberry Grove, reaching Savannah, Georgia, on the evening of Thursday, May 12, 1791.

Saturday, May 14, Washington was waited on by Brethren of the Grand Lodge of Georgia and presented with the following address:[47]

"To the President of the United States.

"*Sir, and Brother,*

"The Grand Master, Officers and Members of the
"Grand Lodge of Georgia, beg leave to congratulate
"you on your arrival in this city. Whilst your ex-
"alted character claims the respect and deference of
"all men, they from the benevolence of masonic prin-
"ciples approach you with the familiar declaration
"of fraternal affection.

"Happy indeed that Society, renowned for its
"antiquity, and pervading influence over the en-
"lightened world, which having ranked a Frederick
"at its head, can now boast of a Washington as a
"Brother. A Brother who it justly hailed the Re-
"deemer of his country, raised it to glory, and by his
"conduct in public and private life has evinced to
"Monarchs that true majesty consists not in splendid
"royalty, but in intrinsic worth.

"With these sentiments they rejoice at your pres-
"ence in this State, and in common with their fellow-

"citizens, greet you, thrice welcome, flattering them-
"selves that your stay will be made agreeable.

"May the great Architect of the Universe pre-
"serve you whilst engaged in the work allotted you
"on earth, and long continue you the brightest pil-
"lar of our Temple, and when the supreme fiat shall
"summon you hence, they pray the might I AM
"may take you into his holy keeping,

      "Grand Lodge in Savannah
May 14th 5791.
Geo: Houston,
Grand Master."

Bro. Washington's Reply to Address from the Grand Lodge of Georgia, May, 1791. Letter Book II, Folio 78.

Upon the next day, Sunday, May 15, after attending the morning church service, Washington left Savannah and set out for Augusta, Georgia, halting for dinner at Mulberry Grove, the seat of Mrs. Nathaniel Greene. The following reply to the Masonic address was sent to the Grand Lodge of Georgia,[48] both address and reply now first published:

"To the Grand Master, Officers and Members
"of the Grand Lodge of Georgia.

"*Gentlemen,*

"I am much obliged by your congratulations
"on my arrival in this city, and I am highly indebted
"to your favorable opinions.

"Every circumstance contributes to
"render my stay in Savannah agreeable, and it
"is cause of regret to me that it must be so
"short.

"My best wishes are offered for the welfare
"of the fraternity, and for your particular happiness.

[signature: G. Washington]

Footnotes:

[47] Washington Letter Book, II, folio 77. Photostat in Archives of the Grand Lodge of Pennsylvania.

[48] Address and Reply, Letter Book II, folio 77-78.

Correspondence with Grand Lodge of Pennsylvania, January 3, 1792.

During the Presidential term of Brother Washington, the President, when in Philadelphia, lived in a large double three-story brick mansion, on the south side of Market Street, sixty feet east of Sixth Street, the site of which is now occupied by three stores, viz.: Nos. 526, 528, 530.

The Grand Lodge of Pennsylvania then held its meetings in the upper floor of the Meeting house of the Free Quakers, still standing, at the southwest corner of Arch and Fifth Streets; this was but a short distance from the presidential mansion. Brother Washington was undoubtedly personally acquainted with many of its members, especially such as had been officers during the Revolution, and were fellow members of the Cincinnati.

On St. John's Day, December 27, 1791, a Grand Lodge was opened in ample form,[49] and the Minutes of the last Grand Communication were read, as far as concerns the election of Grand Officers.

The Grand Officers upon this occasion were:

Brother Jonathan Bayard Smith, *R. W. Grand Master.*

Brother Joseph Few, *Deputy Grand Master.*

Brother Thomas Procter, *Senior Grand Warden.*

Brother Gavin Hamilton, *Junior Grand Warden.*

Brother Peter Le Barbier Duplessis, *Grand Secretary.*

Brother Benjamin Mason, *Grand Treasurer.*

The Rev. Brother Dr. William Smith then addressed the Brethren in an oration suitable to the Grand Day, and the thanks of the Lodge were given to said Brother William Smith for the same.

After which, on motion and seconded, the Rev. Brother Dr. Smith and the Right Worshipful Grand Officers were appointed a Committee to prepare an address to our Illustrious Brother George Washington, President of the United States; and this Lodge was adjourned to the second day of January next to receive the report of said Committee.

"Philadelphia, January 2^d, 1792.

"*Grand Lodge, By Adjournment,*[50]

"A Grand Lodge was opened in ample form, and the Minutes of St. John's Day being read as far as relates to the appointment of a Committee to prepare an Address to our illustrious Brother George Washington, The Rev^d. Bro. D^r. W^m. Smith, one of the said Committee, presented the Draft of one which was read, Whereupon, on Motion and Seconded, the same was unanimously approved of, and Resolved, That the R^t. W^t. Grand Master, Dep^y. G. Master, and Grand Officers, with the Revd Bro. Smith, be a Committee to present the said Address in behalf of this R^t. W^t. Grand Lodge, signed by the Right Worshipful Grand Master, and Countersigned by the Grand Secretary.

"Lodge closed at half past 9 o'clock in Harmony."

Following is the address presented to Brother Washington. Both the original draft in the handwriting of Brother William Smith, showing minor alterations, as well as a fair copy, are in the archives of the Grand Lodge of Pennsylvania.[51]

"To His Excellency George Washington, President of the United States.

"*Sir and Brother.*

"The Ancient *York Masons* of the Jurisdiction of Pennsylvania, for the first time assembled in General

Communication to celebrate the Feast of S^t. John the Evangelist, since your Election to the *Chair* of Government in the United States, beg leave to approach you with Congratulations from the East, and in the pride of Fraternal affection to hail you as the *Great Master Builder* (under the Supreme Architect) by whose labours the *Temple of Liberty* hath been reared in the West, exhibiting to the Nations of the Earth a *Model* of *Beauty*, *Order* and *Harmony* worthy of their Imitation and Praise.

"Your Knowledge of the Origin and Objects of our Institution; its Tendency to promote the Social Affections and harmonize the Heart, give us a sure pledge that this tribute of our Veneration, this Effusion of our Love will not be ungrateful to you; nor will Heaven reject our *Prayer* that you may be long continued to adorn the bright list of Master workmen which our Fraternity in the *terrestrial Lodge*; and that you may be late removed to that *Celestial Lodge* where love and Harmony reign transcendent and Divine; where the great Architect more immediately presides, and where *Cherubim* and *Seraphim*, wafting our Congratulations from *Earth to Heaven*, shall hail you *Brother*.

"By order and in behalf of the Grand Lodge of Pennsylvania in general Communication assembled in Seal) ample form.

"Attest: G^d. Secry.

SIR AND BROTHER:—

The ancient York-Masons of the Jurisdiction of Pennsylvania, for the first Time assembled, in General Communication to celebrate the Feast of St. John the Evangelist, since your Election to the Chair of Government in the United States, beg Leave to approach you, ~~in the Pride of fraternal affection,~~ in the Pride of fraternal affection with Congratulations from the East and, to hail you ~~(under the Supreme Architect)~~ (under the Supreme Architect) as the Great Master-Builder, by whose Labours the Temple of Liberty hath been rear'd in the West, exhibiting to the Nations of the Earth a Model of Beauty Order and Harmony, worthy of their Imitation and Praise.

Your Knowlege of the Origin & Objects of our Institut

on; its Tendency to promote the social affections and harmonize the Heart, gives us a sure Pledge that this Tribute
of our Veneration, this Effusion of our Love, will not be
ungrateful to you; nor will Heaven reject our Prayer
that you may be long continued to adorn the bright List
of Master-Workmen which our Fraternity produces
in the terrestrial Lodge; and that you may be late re-
mov'd to that celestial Lodge where Love & Harmony
reign transcendent and divine; where the Great Architect more immediately presides; and Cherubin & Seraphim
wafting our congratulations from Earth to Heaven, shall
hail you Brother!

Facsimile of the original address read before president Washington by rev. Bro.
William Smith, D.D., January 3, 1792.
Original in archives of Grand Lodge of Pennsylvania. Mss.—volume a.—
folio.—21.

On January 3, 1792, Jonathan Bayard Smith, the Right
Worshipful Grand Master, together with the Grand Officers and
Rev. Brother William Smith called on the President and delivered
the above address.

The deputation was received in the dining room of the
presidential mansion. This was a room about thirty feet long, and
where Washington was accustomed to receive delegations.

At the Quarterly Communication held March 5, 1792, the
Right Worshipful Grand Master Jonathan B. Smith informed the
Brethren that, in conformity to the resolve of this Grand Lodge,
he had, in company with the Grand Officers and the Rev. Brother

D^r. Smith, presented the address to our illustrious Brother George Washington and had received an answer, which was read.

"To the ancient YORK MASONS of the "Jurisdiction of Pennsylvania.

"*Gentlemen and Brothers,*

"I receive your kind Congratulations "with the purest sensations of fraternal affection:—and "from a heart deeply impressed with your generous "wishes for my present and future happiness, I beg "you to accept my thanks.

"At the same time I request you will "be assured of my best wishes and earnest prayers "for your happiness while you remain in this terres- "tial Mansion, and that we may thereafter meet "as brethren in the Eternal Temple of the "Supreme Architect.

To the ancient *York Masons* of the
Jurisdiction of Pennsylvania.

Gentlemen and Brothers,

I receive your kind Congratulations with
the purest sensations of fraternal affection: — And
from a heart deeply impressed with your generous
wishes for my present and future happiness, I beg
you to accept my thanks.

At the same time I request you will
be assured of my best wishes and earnest prayers
for your happiness while you remain in this terrestial Mansion, and that we may thereafter meet
as brethren in the Eternal Temple of the
Supreme Architect.

G. Washington

*Facsimile of Washington's Reply to Grand Lodge of Pennsylvania, January,
1792. Original in Archives of the Grand Lodge.*

Whereupon, on motion and seconded, Resolved,
unanimously, that the said address and the answer thereto, shall be
entered on the minutes.

This answer, in possession of the Grand Lodge of Pennsylvania, is in the handwriting of Tobias Lear, who was the private secretary of the President, and for years attended to the details of Washington's domestic affairs, and was liberally remembered by him in his will.

The letter was signed by Washington, who had both the address and answer copied verbatim in one of his letter books[52] by Bartholomew Dandridge, secretary to the President. A photostat copy of above, together with the original answer by Washington is in the Archives of the Grand Lodge of Pennsylvania.

This address was read by Rev. Brother William Smith, one of the most noted Episcopal preachers in Philadelphia, and the first Provost of the College of Philadelphia, now the University of Pennsylvania. Brother William Smith, D.D., had been an active member of the Masonic Fraternity in Pennsylvania for forty years; he was the Chaplain of the Grand Lodge of Moderns for almost a quarter of a century. In winter of 1778 he joined the Grand Lodge of Ancient York Masons, and for some time served as Grand Secretary.[53]

Jonathan Bayard Smith, the Grand Master of Pennsylvania, was one of Philadelphia's prominent citizens. During the Revolutionary period he was an ardent patriot; he was among the earliest of those who espoused the cause of independence. In 1775 he was chosen secretary of the Committee of Safety, and in February, 1777, he was elected by the assembly a delegate to the Continental Congress. He was a second time chosen to this post, serving in the congresses of 1777-8. From April 4, 1777, till Nov. 13, 1778, he was prothonotary of the court of Common Pleas.

On December 1, 1777, he presided at the public meeting, in Philadelphia, of "Real Whigs," by whom it was resolved "That it be recommended to the council of safety that in this great emergency ... every person between the age of sixteen and fifty years be ordered out under arms." During this year he was commissioned lieutenant-colonel of a battalion of "Associators."

In 1778 he was appointed a justice of the court of Common Pleas, Quarter Sessions, and Orphans' Court, which post he held for many years. He was appointed in 1781, one of the auditors of the accounts of Pennsylvania troops in the service of the United States. In 1792, and subsequently, he was chosen an alderman of the city, which was an office of great dignity in his day, and in 1794 he was elected auditor-general of Pennsylvania.

Brother Jonathan B. Smith was an active member of the Grand Lodge of Pennsylvania. He was the Senior Grand Warden in 1786, at the time when the Provincial Grand Lodge of Pennsylvania: "*Resolved*, that the Grand Lodge is, and ought to be perfectly independent and free of any such foreign jurisdiction."[54]

In the two following years he was appointed Deputy Grand Master by Right Worshipful Grand Master William Adcock; he was elected Right Worshipful Grand Master in 1789 and served in that capacity for six years (1789-1794). In the year 1798 he was again elected to that honorable office, serving five more consecutive years (1798 to 1802), when he declined reëlection. The following action was taken by the Grand Lodge:[55]

"On Motion made and Seconded the Grand Lodge of Pennsylvania impressed with a grateful sense of the long assiduous and highly useful labours of their late R. W. Grand Master, Bro[r] Jonathan Bayard Smith, Esqr, previous to and during his service in the high Station which he has left, Resolved Unanimously, That the most respectful Thanks of the said G. Lodge be presented to their said Brother Jonathan Bayard Smith for the eminent services he has rendered to the Craft generally and more especially for the able, diligent and impartial manner in which he has discharged the Duties of the Chair and while they deplore the necessity of his now retiring from the Official Station amongst them which he has so Honourably filled, they hope for a continuance of his Brotherly Love, Aid and information and finally that he be requested to receive the best wishes of the Grand Lodge for a prolongation of his useful life, a commensurate enjoyment of his Health and his final Happiness in the Mansion of Everlasting Rest."

Brother Joseph Few, Deputy Grand Master, was also a Revolutionary Soldier, having served as Regimental Quarter Master with the 4th Continental Artillery.

Brother Thomas Procter, Senior Grand Warden, formerly Colonel of the Pennsylvania Artillery, and Warrant Master of the Military Lodge, No. 19, upon the Roster of Pennsylvania was prominent in both civil and political affairs during Washington's administration. A full account of Brother Thomas Procter and this Military Lodge will be found in the History of the Old Masonic Lodges of Pennsylvania, published by the Grand Lodge in 1913.[56]

For a sketch of Brother Peter Le Barbier Duplessis, the reader is referred to the same volume.[57]

Footnotes:

[49] Reprint of Minutes of Grand Lodge of Pennsylvania, Vol. I, p. 178.

[50] *Ibid.*, p. 180.

[51] Mss. Volume A, folio 17, 19, 21.

[52] Letter Book II, pp. 104-105.

[53] Cf. "Old Masonic Lodges of Pennsylvania," Vol. I, p. 201.

[54] Cf. Reprint of Minutes of Grand Lodge, Vol. I, p. 96 *et seq.*

[55] *Ibid.*, Vol. II, p. 68.

[56] Volume II, Chapter XXVI, pp. 1-36. Cf. also "Freemasonry in Pennsylvania," Vol. I and II, for various references to Col. Procter.

[57] Cf. "Old Lodges," Vol. II, pp. 256 *et seq.*

Correspondence with Grand Lodge of Massachusetts, December, 1792.

"At Grand Lodge held at Concert Hall, Boston, 10th of December, 5792, being a Quarterly Communication it was

"*Resolved*, That the Grand Master, with the Grand Wardens, present to our Most Beloved Brother

George Washington, the new Book of Constitutions, with a suitable address."

At the next Quarterly Communication we find that,

"Agreeably to a resolve at the last Quarterly Communication, the Grand Master, with his Wardens, reported:

"That they had written to our beloved President and Brother, George Washington, and presented him with a Book of Constitutions, to which letter he had been pleased to make answer. The letter and answer were read, and Voted to be inserted in the records of the Grand Lodge."

This address was evidently sent to President Washington at Philadelphia, and was answered from the presidential office in that city. No date nor place appears upon either the original so far as known, nor the copy in the letter book, both address and reply therein being in the handwriting of Bartholomew Dandridge, Secretary to the President.

The following copy of both address and reply are taken from Letter Book II, folio 106-108.

"An Address of the Grand Lodge of Free &
"Accepted Masons for the Commonwealth
"of Massachusetts, To their honored and

Julius F. Sachse

"Illustrious Brother.

GEORGE WASHINGTON.

"Whilst the Historian is describing the
"career of your glory, and the inhabitants
"of an extensive Empire are made happy
"in your unexampled exertions:—whilst some
"celebrate the Hero so distinguished in li-
"berating United America; and others the Patriot
"who presides over her Councils, a Band of bro-
"thers, having always joined the acclamations
"of their countrymen, now testify their res-
"pect for those milder virtues which have
"ever graced the man.

"Taught by the precepts of our Society;
"that all its members *stand upon a level*, we
"venture to assume this station & to approach
"you with that freedom which diminishes
"our diffidence without lessening our respect.

"Desirous to enlarge the boundaries of
"social happiness, and to vindicate the cere-
"monies of their institution, this Grand Lodge
"have published a "Book of Constitutions," (and
"a copy for your acceptance accompanies
"this) which by discovering the principles that
"actuate will speak the Eulogy of the Society;
"though they fervently wish the conduct of its;
"Members may prove its higher commendation.

"Convinced of his attachment to its
"cause, and readiness to encourage its bene-

"volent designs; they have taken the liberty to
"dedicate this work to one, the qualities of
"whose heart and the actions of whose life
"have contributed to improve personal virtue,
"and extend throughout the world, the most endear-
"ing cordialities; and they humbly hope he will
"pardon this freedom, and accept the tribute of
"their esteem & homage.

"May the supreme architect of the uni-
"verse protect & bless you, give you length of
"days & increase of Felicity in this world, and then
"receive you to the harmonious & exalted So-
"ciety in Heaven.—

      "John   *Gran*
Cutler,   *d Master*

      "Josiah
Bartlett   *Gr^d*
"Mungo Machey   *Wardens.*

      "Boston
"Decem. 27, A.D. 1792."

The following reply was sent by President Washington from Philadelphia to the Brethren of the Grand Lodge of Massachusetts. It will be noticed that there was no date or place mentioned upon the copy in the Letter Book, nor on the original letter, which at present is believed to be in the Library of the Grand Lodge of Massachusetts.

Washington's Reply

"To the Grand Lodge of Free & accepted Ma-
"sons, For the Commonwealth of Massachu-
"setts.

"Flattering as it may be to the human
"mind, & truly honorable as it is to receive
"from our fellow citizens testimonies of appro-
"bation for exertions to promote the public wel-
"fare, it is not less pleasing to know, that the
"milder virtues of the heart are highly respected
"by a Society whose liberal principles must be
"founded in the immutable laws of truth and
"justice.—

"To enlarge the sphere of social happi-
"ness is worthy the benevolent design of a ma-
"sonic institution; and it is most fervently to
"be wished, that the conduct of every member
"of the fraternity, as well as those publications
"that discover the principles which actuate them;
"may tend to convince mankind that the grand
"object of Masonry is to promote the happiness
"of the human race.

"While I beg your acceptance of
"my thanks for the "Book of Constitutions" which
"you have sent me, & the honor you have done
"me in the dedication, permit me to assure you
"that I feel all those emotions of gratitude
"which your affectionate address & cordial
"wishes are calculated to inspire; and I
"sincerely pray that the Great Architect
"of the Universe may bless you here, and
"receive you hereafter into his immortal Temple.

No facsimile copy of the original letter was obtainable for the Collection of the Grand Lodge of Pennsylvania.

To the Grand Lodge of Free & accepted Masons for the Commonwealth of Massachusetts —

Flattering as it may be to the human mind, & truly honorable as it is to receive from our fellow Citizens testimonies of approbation for exertions to promote the public welfare—, it is not less pleasing to know, that the milder virtues of the heart are highly respected by a Society whose liberal principles must be founded in the immutable Laws of truth and justice.—

To enlarge the sphere of social happiness is worthy the benevolent design of a masonic Institution; and it is most fervently to be wished, that the conduct of every member of the fraternity, as well as those publications that discover the principles which actuate them may tend to convince mankind that the grand object of masonry is to promote the happiness of the human race.

While I beg your acceptance of my thanks for the "Book of Constitutions" which you have sent me, & the honor you have done me in the dedication, permit me to assure you that I feel all those emotions of gratitude which your affectionate address & cordial wishes are calculated to inspire; and I sincerely pray that the Great Architect of the Universe may bless you here, and receive you hereafter into his immortal Temple.

G. Washington

Washington's Reply to the Grand Lodge of Massachusetts. Letter Book II, Folio 108.

Correspondence with Grand Lodge of Pennsylvania, December, 1796.

September 18, 1796, President Washington issued his farewell address. His second term was drawing to a close; the term had been a more or less exciting one: The passing of the Neutrality Act; Genet's appeal from the executive to the people; the Fugitive Slave Act; the whiskey insurrection in western Pennsylvania; the adoption of the Eleventh amendment; the purchase of peace from Algiers, Tripoli and Tunis; the troubles with Great Britain about the non-delivery of the military posts and later the Jay Treaty, all came within President Washington's second and last term.[58]

During these troublous times Washington had no stauncher supporters than his Masonic Brethren of the Grand Lodge of Pennsylvania. Further, that Washington kept more or less in touch with his Masonic Brethren of the Grand Lodge of Pennsylvania is shown by the fact that he attended the services at St. Paul's Episcopal Church, on Third Street below Walnut, on St. John's Day, December 27, 1793, where a charity sermon was preached by Rev. Brother Samuel Magaw, D.D., Vice-Provost of the University of Pennsylvania, before the Grand and Subordinate Lodges for the purpose of increasing the relief fund, for the widows and orphans of the yellow fever epidemic which ravaged the capital city during the past summer.[59]

When the Brethren found that Washington positively declined reëlection in 1796, and that John Adams was elected to succeed him on the fourth of March following, the Brethren of the Grand Lodge at their Quarterly Communication, December 5, 1796, determined that it would be right and proper to present him with an address before his retirement from office, whereupon, it was resolved: "On Motion and seconded, that a Committee be appointed to frame an Address to be presented on the ensuing Feast of St John, Decem^r 27th, to the Great Master Workman, our

Illustrious Br. Washington, on the occasion of his intended retirement from Public Labor, to be also laid before the said Grand Lodge on St John's Day, and the R^t W. Grand Master, Deputy G. M. B^{rs} Sadler, Milnor and Williams, were accordingly appointed."

At a Grand Lodge held on St. John's Day, Philadelphia, December 27, 5796, "The Committee appointed to prepare an Address to our Brother George Washington, President of the United States, presented an Address by them drawn up, which was ordered to be read, and was in the words following, to wit:

"To George Washington President of The United States.

"The Address of the Grand Lodge of Pennsyl-
"vania.

"*Most Respected Sir and Brother,*

"Having announced your intention to retire from
"*Public Labour* to that *Refreshment* to which your
"preëminent Services for near Half a Century have
"so justly entitled you. Permit the Grand Lodge
"of Pennsylvania at this last Feast of our Evangelic
"Master St. John, on which we can hope for an im-
"mediate Communication with you to join the grate-
"ful Voice of our Country in Acknowledging that
"you have carried forth the Principles of the Lodge
"into every Walk of your Life, by your constant
"Labours for the Prosperity of that Country, by
"your unremitting Endeavours to promote Order,
"Union and Brotherly Affection amongst us, and
"lastly by the Vows of your Farewell Address to
"your Brethren and Fellow Citizens. An Address
"which we trust Our Children and Our Childrens
"Children will ever look upon as a most invaluable
"Legacy from a *Friend* a *Benefactor* and a *Father*.

"To these our grateful Acknowledgments (leav-
"ing to the impartial Pen of History to record the
"important Events in which you have borne so illus-
"trious a part) permit us to add our most fervent
"prayers, that after enjoying to the utmost of
"Human Life, every Felicity which the Terrestial
"Lodge can afford, you may be received by the
"great Master Builder of this World and of Worlds
"unnumbered, into the Ample Felicity of that *Celes-*
"*tial Lodge* in which alone distinguished Virtues and
"distinguished Labours can be eternally rewarded.

"By unanimous order of the Grand Lodge of
"Pennsylvania at their communication held the 27th
"Day of December Anno Domini 5796.

It was then moved and seconded that the same be
adopted. Upon the question being taken it appeared that it was
approved of. On motion and seconded, it was agreed that a
committee be appointed to wait on Brother Washington to
acquaint him that it is the intention of this Grand Lodge to
present an address to him, and to know what time he shall be
pleased to appoint to receive it. The committee appointed to
perform this duty were Brothers William Smith, Peter Le Barbier
Duplessis and Thomas Procter, who, after having waited on him,
reported that he had appointed to-morrow, December 28, 1796, at
twelve o'clock to receive it. Said committee, to wit, Brothers W.
Smith, Duplessis and Procter, together with Right Worshipful

Grand Master, Deputy Grand Master, and Junior Wardens, Grand
Secretary and the Masters of the different Lodges in the City, were
then appointed a Deputation to present the said Address.

This deputation consisted of Right Worshipful Grand
Master William Moore Smith, Gavin Hamilton, Deputy Grand
Master, Thomas Town, Senior Grand Warden, Thomas
Armstrong, Esqr., Junior Grand Warden, George A. Baker, Grand
Secretary, John McElwee, Grand Treasurer, and the following
Masters of the Philadelphia Lodges, viz.: David Irwin, No. 2,
Israel Israel, No. 3, Andrew Nilson No. 9, Eleaser Oswald, No.
19, Cadawalder Griffith, No. 52, Richard E. Cusack, No. 59,
Thomas Bradley, No. 67, William Nelson, No. 71; together with
the appointed Committee, Brothers William Smith D.D., Le
Barbier Duplessis and Thomas Procter.

President Washington received the august deputation of
the Brethren at the appointed time; the address was read before
him by the Rev. Brother William Smith, D.D., whereupon he
returned them a reply. This document, still in the Library of the
Grand Lodge of Pennsylvania, is entirely in the handwriting of
Washington and signed by him, viz.:

"Fellow-citizens and Brothers,
"of the Grand Lodge of Pennsylvania.

"I have received your address
"with all the feelings of brotherly affection,
"mingled with those sentiments, for the
"Society, which it was calculated to excite.

"To have been, in any degree, an
"instrument in the hands of Providence,
"to promote order and union, and erect upon
"a solid foundation the true principles of
"government, is only to have shared with
"many others in a labour, the result of

"which let us hope, will prove through
"all ages, a sanctuary for brothers and
"a lodge for the virtues,—

"Permit me to reciprocate your
"prayers for my temporal happiness,
"and to supplicate that we may all
"meet thereafter in that eternal temple,
"whose builder is the great architect
"of the Universe.

Fellow-citizens and Brothers,
of the Grand Lodge of Pennsylvania

I have received your address with all the feelings of brotherly affection, mingled with those sentiments, for the Society, which it was calculated to excite.

To have been, in any degree, an instrument in the hands of Providence, to promote order and union, and erect upon a solid foundation the true principles of government, is only to have shared with many others in a labour, the result of which let us hope, will prove through all ages, a sanctuary for brothers and a lodge for the virtues. —

Permit me to reciprocate your prayers for my temporal happiness, and to supplicate that we may all meet thereafter in that eternal temple, whose builder is the great architect of the Universe

G Washington

Facsimile of Washington's Reply to Grand Lodge of Pennsylvania, December, 1796. Original in Archives of the Grand Lodge of Pennsylvania.

Brother William Moore Smith, Right Worshipful Grand Master of Pennsylvania, whose first official act as Grand Master was to head the committee to call on the President, was a son of the Rev. William Smith, D.D., born in Philadelphia, June 1, 1759. He was a lawyer by profession and served as Deputy Grand Master for the year 1795 under the Venerable William Ball, and as Right Worshipful Grand Master for the years 1796-1797. He was appointed by the President as agent for the settlement of claims that were provided for in the Sixth Article of John Jay's Treaty, and visited England in 1803 to close the commission. He died at the Smith Homestead at Falls of Schuylkill, March 12, 1821.

Both the address and reply were copied in Washington's Letter Book III, pp. 244-245, in the handwriting of one of his secretaries, G. W. Craik, a son of Dr. James Craik, Washington's "compatriot in arms, and old and intimate friend," who attended him during his last illness.

Photostat copies of above are in the Library of the Grand Lodge of Pennsylvania, also the original draft of the address, presented to the President (Mss. Volume A, folio 23).

This autograph Masonic letter from Washington to the Grand Lodge of Pennsylvania has been reproduced in facsimile, published and circulated (in most cases without the knowledge or consent of the Grand Lodge of Pennsylvania) more widely than any other known letter of Washington. Some of these copies are treasured by their owners under the impression that they have the original letter. Several cases of this kind have of late come under the notice of the writer. In one case where one of these reproductions was offered for sale, hundreds of dollars were asked for the reproduction, and it was with great difficulty that the owner could be convinced of its character.

Another use made of this letter by unprincipled persons was to make a photo-lithographic copy of the letter, and substitute the name of another state for that of Pennsylvania, and then palm it off upon the authorities of that state as an original letter to their Grand Lodge. The latest case of this kind known to the writer is that of the Grand Lodge of Georgia, who were thus imposed upon.

Then again the letter has been extensively used for advertising purposes by publishing houses of Masonic literature.

The letter has also been printed in most all books bearing upon Masonic history during the revolutionary period.

It was also frequently quoted and criticised during the Anti-Masonic craze which swept over the country some eighty-odd years ago, it being the chief Masonic letter of the five known to the leaders of those misguided persons. The main point of their argument was that it bore no date and therefore was not authentic.

Footnotes:

[58] Cf. The Religious and Social Conditions of Philadelphia, under the Federal Constitution, 1790-1800. Julius F. Sachse, Philadelphia, 1900.

[59] Cf. "Freemasonry in Pennsylvania," before quoted, Vol. II, pp. 190-197; original copy in archives of Grand Lodge of Pennsylvania.

Correspondence with Alexandria Lodge, No. 22, Virginia.

Upon pages 244 and 245 of Washington's folio Letter Book No. III in the Library of Congress are recorded a letter and address to Washington from the Master of Alexandria Lodge, No. 22, of Virginia, together with Washington's reply.

Washington and his family had left Philadelphia, Thursday, March 9, 1797, for Mount Vernon, and arrived at Baltimore, Sunday, March 12, and at Mount Vernon, March 15, where he again settled down to the life of a private gentleman, free from the cares and concerns of public life.

March 28, 1797, he was waited on at Mount Vernon by Brothers Dennis Ramsay and Phillip G. Marsteller, and presented with the following letter and address from James Gillies, the Master of Alexandria Lodge, No. 22, of Virginia, viz.:

"Alex^A March 28th, 5797.

"*Most respected Brother*,

"Brother Ramsay & Marsteller wait upon you "with a copy of an address which has been prepared "by the unanimous desire of the Ancient York Ma- "sons of Lodge No. 22. It is their earnest request "that you will partake of a Dinner with them and "that you will please appoint the time most conve- "nient for you to attend.—

"I am most beloved Brother,
"Your Mo. Ob^t H^{ble} Servt
"James Gillies, *M.*

"Genl Geo Washington."

The letter was an invitation to dine with the Lodge. This Washington accepted.

"*Most respected Brother*,

"The ancient York Masons of Lodge No. 22 offer you "their warmest congratulations on your retire-
"ment from your useful labors. Under the su-
"preme architect of the Universe you have been the "Master Workman in erecting the Temple of Lib-
"erty in the west, on the broad basis of equal rights. "In your wise administration of the government of "the United States for the space of eight years, you "have kept within the compass of our happy Consti-
"tution and acted on the square with foreign Na-
"tions and thereby preserved your country in peace "and promoted the prosperity and happiness of your "fellow Citizens, and now that you have retired from "the labours of public life to the refreshment of "domestic tranquility, they ardently pray that you "may long enjoy all the happiness which the Terres-
"tial Lodge can afford and finally be removed to that "celestial Lodge where Love, Peace and Harmony "for ever reign and where cherubims and seraphims "shall hail you Brother.—

"By the unanimous desire of Lodge
"No. 22
"James Gillies, *Master*."

"Gen Geo Washington."

Washington attended the meeting of his Lodge at Alexandria, on Saturday, April 1, 1797, when his reply to Brother Gillies' address was read in open Lodge, viz.:

"Brothers of the Ancient York Masons of Lodge No. 22.

"While my heart acknowledges with Brotherly "Love, your affectionate congratulations on my re-"tirement from the arduous toils of past years, my "gratitude is no less excited by your kind wishes for "my future happiness.—

"If it has pleased the supreme architect of the "universe to make me an humble instrument to pro-"mote the welfare and happiness of my fellow men, "my exertions have been abundantly recompensed "by the kind partiality with which they have been "received; and the assurance you give me of your "belief that I have acted upon the square in my "public capacity, will be among my principles en-"joyments in this Terrestial Lodge.

Ala.ª March 28, 1797

Most respected Brother,

*Brother Ramsay & Master will wait
upon you with a copy of an address which has been prepared
by the unanimous desire of the ancient York Masons of Lodge
Nº 22. It is their earnest request that you will partake of
a Dinner with them, and that you will please appoint the
time most convenient, for you to attend. —*

*I am most hon'd Brother
Your Bro. & hble Serv*

Gen'l Geo Washington   *James Gillis, M.*

*Facsimile of Letter from W. M. of Alexandria Lodge to Bro. Washington,
March, 1797. Letter Book II, Folio 294.*

Most respected Brother,

The ancient york Masons of Lodge Nº 22 offer you their warmest congratulations on your retirement from your useful labors — Under the supreme architect of the Universe you have been the master workman in erecting the Temple of Liberty in the west on the broad basis of equal rights — In your wise administration of the government of the United States for the space of eight years, you have kept within the Compass of our happy Constitution and acted on the square with foreign nations and thereby preserved your country in peace and promoted the prosperity and happiness of your fellow Citizens, and now that you have retired from the labours of public life to the refreshment of domestic tranquility, they ardently pray that you may long enjoy all the happiness which the Terrestrial Lodge can afford and finally be removed to that celestial Lodge where Love, Peace, and Harmony for ever reign and where Cherubims and seraphims shall hail you Brother —

By the unanimous desire of Lodge Nº 22

James Gilless, Master

Gen Geo. Washington

Facsimile of Address from Alexandria Lodge, No. 22, to Washington, March, 1797. Letter Book II, Folio 294-295.

Facsimile of Washington's Reply to Alexandria Lodge, No. 22, Virginia, March, 1797.

After which the Brethren went in procession from their room to Abert's Tavern,[60] where they partook of an "elegant" dinner, following which a number of toasts were offered. The tenth toast was by Brother Washington, "The Lodge at Alexandria, and all Masons throughout the World," after which he returned to Mount Vernon under an escort of mounted troops of the town.[61]

The copies of the letter, address and reply in Washington's Letter Book are in the handwriting of his secretary, Tobias Lear. Photostats of all are in the collection of the Grand Lodge of Pennsylvania. No direct photograph of the original in possession of Alexandria-Washington Lodge, No. 22, was obtainable.

Footnotes:

[60] Abert's Tavern, formerly "John Wise's." *Vide* p. 35 *supra*.

[61] Cf. "Washington after the Revolution," W. S. Baker, p. 347.

Correspondence With Grand Lodge of Massachusetts, March, 1797.

At a Grand Lodge in Quarterly Communication, held at Concert Hall, Boston, on the evening of March 18, A.L. 5797.

"On motion it was Voted, That a committee be appointed to draft an Address, to be presented to our Illustrious Brother, George Washington, Esq'r, when the M.W. Paul Revere, Grand Master, R.W. John Warren, Rev. Bro. Thaddeus M. Harris, R.W. Josiah Bartlett, Bro. Thomas Edwards, were appointed a committee for that purpose."

In response to above resolution the following address was sent to Brother Washington at Mount Vernon dated Boston, March 21, 5797, viz.:

"The East, the West and the South, of the Grand Lodge of Free and Accepted Masons of the Commonwealth of Massachusetts.

To Their Most Worthy George Washington."

"Wishing ever to be foremost in testimonials of respect and admiration for those virtues and services with which you have so long adorned and benefited our common country; and not the last nor least, to regret the cessation of them, in the public councils of the Union; your Brethren of the Grand Lodge embrace the earliest opportunity of greeting you in the calm retirement you have contemplated to yourself. Though as citizens they lose you in the active labors of political life, they hope, as Masons, to find you in the pleasing sphere of Fraternal engagement.

"From the cares of state and the fatigues of public business our institution opens a recess affording all the relief of tranquility, the harmony of peace and the refreshment of pleasure.

Of these may you partake in all their purity and satisfaction; and we will assure ourselves that your attachment to this social plan will increase; and that under the auspices of your encouragement, assistance and patronage, the Craft will attain its highest ornament, perfection and praise. And it is our ardent prayer, that when your light shall be no more visible in this earthly temple, you may be raised to the All Perfect Lodge above; be seated on the right of the Supreme Architect of the Universe, and there receive the refreshment your labors merited.

"In behalf of the Grand Lodge, we subscribe ourselves with the highest esteem,

"Your affectionate Brethren,
"Paul Revere, *Grand Master.*
"Isaiah Thomas, *S. Grand Warden.*
"Joseph Laughton, *J. Grand Warden.*
"Daniel Oliver, Grand Secretary,
"Boston, 21st March, 5797."

For some unaccountable reason the delivery of the address was delayed and not received at Mount Vernon until late in April. The original draft of Washington's reply to the Grand Lodge of Massachusetts in his own handwriting and signature as well as an autograph note of apology for the seeming delay to Grand Master Paul Revere and his officers dated Mount Vernon, April 24, 1797, are in the Manuscript Department in the Library of Congress, viz.:

"To Paul Revere Grand Master, Isaiah
"Thomas Senior Grand Warden and
"Joseph Laughton Junr Grand Warden.

"*Brothers,*

"I am sorry that the en-
"closed answer to the affectionate address
"of the Grand Lodge of Ancient, Free and

"Accepted Masons, of the Commonwealth
"of Massachusetts transmitted under your
"signatures, should appear so much out
from
"of season; but ^ the lapse of time between
"the date & reception of the address (from
"what cause I know not) it was not to be
"avoided, and is offered as an apology, for
"the delay. With brotherly affection

    "I am always yours,

"Mount Vernon,
24th April 1797."

To Paul Revere Grand Master, Isaiah Thomas Senior Grand Warden and Joseph Laughton Jun.r Grand Warden

Brothers;

I am sorry that the enclosed answer to the affectionate address of the Grand Lodge of Ancient, Free and accepted Masons, of the Commonwealth of Massachusetts. transmitted under your signatures. should appear so much out of season.; but The lapse of time between the date & reception of the Address (from what cause I know not) it was not to be avoided, and is offered as an apology for the delay — With brotherly affection I am always Yours

G. Washington

Mount Vernon.
24.th April 1797.

Facsimile of Autograph Letter from Washington to Paul Revere and the
Officers of the Grand Lodge of Massachusetts, April 24, 1797.

April 1797

To the Grand Lodge of ancient, Free &
accepted Masons, of the Commonwealth
of Massachusetts.

Brothers,

It was not until within
these few days that I have been favoured by
the receipt of your affectionate address.
dated in Boston the 21st of March

For the favourable sentiments
you have been pleased to express on the
occasion of my past services, and for the
regrets with which they are accompani
ed for the cessation of my public functions,
I pray you to accept my best acknowledg
ments and gratitude. _

No pleasure except that wch
results from a consciousness of having, to
the utmost of my abilities, discharged
the trusts which have been reposed in
me by my Country, can equal the satis
faction I feel from the unequivocal proof
I continually receive of its approbation
of my public conduct, and I beg you to be
assured that the evidence thereof which

is

*Facsimile of Original Draft of Washington's Reply to the Address from the
Grand Lodge of Massachusetts in Library of Congress.*

Following is a copy of Washington's original draft of his
reply to the Grand Lodge of Massachusetts. It is written upon two
pages of a letter sheet entirely in his handwriting and signed by
him.

"To the Grand Lodge of Ancient, Free &
"Accepted Masons, of the Commonwealth
"of Massachusetts.

"*Brothers,*

"It was not until within
"these few days that I have been favoured by
"the receipt of your affectionate Address
"dated in Boston the 21st of March

"For the favourable sentiments
"you have been pleased to express on the
"occasion of my past services, and for the
"regrets with which they are accompani-
"ed for the cessation of my public functions,
"I pray you to accept my best acknowledg-
"ments and gratitude.—

"No pleasure, except that w^{ch}
"results from a consciousness of having, to
"the utmost of my abilities, discharged,
"the trusts which have been reposed in
"me by my Country, can equal the satis
"faction I feel from the unequivocal proofs
"I continually receive of its approbation
"of my public conduct, and I beg you to be
"assured that the evidence thereof which
"is exhibited by the Grand Lodge of Massachusetts
"is not among the least pleasing, or grate
"ful to my feelings.—

"In that retirement which decli-
"ning years induced me to seek, and which
"repose, to a mind long employed in pub-
"lic concerns, rendered necessary, my wish

"es that bounteous Providence will conti-
"nue to bless & preserve our country in
"Peace & in the prosperity it has enjoyed, will
"be warm & sincere; and my attachment
"to the Society of which we are members
"will dispose me always, to contribute my best
"endeavours to promote the honor &
"interest of the *Craft.*—

"For the prayer you offer in
"my behalf I entreat you to accept the
"thanks of a grateful heart; with the as-
"surance of fraternal regard and best
"wishes for the honor, happiness & prospe-
"rity of all the members of the Grand Lodge
"of Massachusetts.

G. Washington

The original letter is said to be in possession of the Grand
Lodge of Massachusetts. No photographic facsimile of the
document, however, could be obtained.

Correspondence with Grand Lodge of Maryland, November, 1798.

In the year 1798, the danger of a war with France had become so imminent, on account of the aggressions of that government towards the United States, that Congress ordered a provisional army to be raised, the command of which was tendered to Washington, with the rank of Lieutenant-General, an honor which was reluctantly accepted by Washington. During the summer a scourge of yellow fever had again visited Philadelphia, which caused Congress to adjourn, July 16, and the public offices to be removed for the time being to Trenton, N. J. All danger of the fever being over, Washington, on November 5, started for Trenton. He arrived at Baltimore, November 7, and was waited on at his quarters by William Belton, Grand Master of the Grand Lodge of Maryland, his Deputy and other Brethren and presented with a copy of the New Ahiman Rezon and the following address,[62] viz.:

"To George Washington, Esq.,
Lieutenant General and Commander-in-chief of the Armies of the United States.

"*Sir and Brother:*

"The Right Worshipful Grand Lodge of Free Masons for the State of Maryland, wishing to testify the respect in which the whole fraternity in this State hold the man who is at once the ornament of the Society and of his country, vote a copy of the Constitution of Masonry, lately printed under its authority, to be presented to you.

"Accept, Sir and Brother, from our hands this small token of the veneration of men who consider it as the greatest boast of their Society, that a WASHINGTON openly avows himself a member of it, and thinks it worthy of his approbation. With it accept also our warmest congratulations in the name of the body which we represent, on your reappointment to that elevated station in which you formerly wrought the salvation of your country; and on your restoration to the inestimable blessing of health which, that the Almighty disposer of events may continue to accord to you uninterruptedly, is the most earnest prayer of your most respectfully affectionate Brethren and most humble servants.

"Signed, Wm. Belton, R.. W..G..M..
"Peter Little, Grand Secretary,
"Baltimore, November 5th, 1798."

To the Right Worshipful Grand Lodge 1798
Masons for the State of Maryland

Gentlemen & Brothers

Your obliging & affectionate
Letter, together with a Copy of the Constitution of
Masonary has been put into my hands by
your Provincial Master; for which I pray you
accept my best thanks.

acquainted with the principles of doctrine of
Free Masonary, I am sure to be
in benevolence and to be excused
for the Good of Mankind,

Facsimile (reduced) of the original draft of Washington's letter to the grand lodge of Maryland.—Elkton, MD., Nov. 8, 1798.

To this address Washington sent a reply, the original draft of which is in the Library of Congress, written upon two pages of a letter sheet, and differs somewhat from the final copy sent to the Grand Lodge from Elkton, where Washington spent the next day. It will be recalled that but two weeks had elapsed since he wrote his last letter to Dominie Snyder of Fredericktown, and this fact was evidently in his mind when he wrote this letter to the Maryland Brethren.

Upon second thought he eliminated the lines bearing upon the insinuations in Snyder's letter. Following is a copy of the letter as originally written, viz.:

"To the Right Worshipful Grand Lodge of Free
"Masons for the State of Maryland.

"*Gentlemen & Brothers,*

"Your obliging & affectionate
"letter, together with a copy of the Constitutions of
"Masonry has been put into my hands by
"your Grand Master; for which I pray you to
"accept my best thanks.—
"So far as I am
"acquainted with the principles & Doctrines of
"Free Masonry, I conceive it to be founded
"in benevolence and to be exercised only
"for the good of mankind. *If it has been a*
"*Cloak to promote improper or nefarious*
"*objects, it is a melancholly proof that*
"*in unworthy hands, the best institutions*
"*may be made use of to promote the worst*
"*designs.—*

"While I offer my grateful
"acknowledgements for your congratulations on my
"late appointments, and for the favorable sentiments

"you are pleased to express of my conduct, permit

"me to observe, that at this important &

"critical moment, when repeated and

"high indignities have been offered to this

"government your country and the rights & property

"of our Citizens plundered without a prospect of

"redress, I conceive it to be the *indispensable*

"duty of every American, let his situation & cir

"cumstances in life be what they may, to come

"forward in support of the government of his country

"and to give all the aid in his power toward

"maintaining that independence which we have

"so dearly purchased; and under this impression,

"I did not hesitate to lay aside all personal

"considerations and accept my appointment.

"I pray you to be assured that I ap-

"preciate, with sincerity your kind wishes for

"my health & happiness.

     "I am Gentl^n & brothers

"very respectfully

"Yr most ob^t serv^t."

Before this letter was sent, the five words on the tenth line and the whole of next five lines were eliminated; there was also a slight change made in the last paragraph on the second page.

Following is a copy of the letter as received by the Grand Lodge of Maryland. The original letter was in the possession of

the Grand Lodge of Maryland, as late as 1833, but it has since disappeared.[63]

"To the Right Worshipful Grand Lodge of Free Masons for the State of Maryland.

"*Gentlemen and Brothers:*

"Your obliging and affectionate letter, together with a copy of the Constitution of Masonry, has been put into my hands by your Grand Master, for which I pray you to accept my best thanks. So far as I am acquainted with the principles and doctrines of Freemasonry, I conceive them to be founded on benevolence, and to be exercised for the good of mankind; I cannot, therefore, upon this ground withdraw my approbation from it.

"While I offer my grateful acknowledgements for your congratulations on my late appointment, and for the favorable sentiments you are pleased to express of my conduct, permit me to observe, that, at this important and critical moment, when high and repeated indignities have been offered to the Government of our country, and when the property of our citizens is plundered without a prospect of redress, I conceive it to be the indispensable duty of every American, let his station and circumstances in life be what they may, to come forward in support of the Government of his choice and to give all the aid in his power towards maintaining that independence which we have so dearly purchased; and under this impression, I did not hesitate to lay aside all personal considerations and accept my appointment. I pray you to be assured that I receive with gratitude your kind wishes for my health and happiness and reciprocate them with sincerity.

"I am, Gentlemen and Brothers,
"Very Respectfully,
"Your most Ob't Servant,

"Elkton, November 8th, 1798."

Footnotes:

[62] Cf. "Freemasonry in Maryland," by Edw. J. Schultz, Baltimore, 1884, Vol. I, pp. 265-266.

[63] *Ibid.*, p. 266.

Correspondence with G. W. Snyder, 1798.

As to the correspondence with one G. W. Snyder (Schneider), who represented himself as a preacher of the Reformed Church of Fredericktown, Maryland, our late Brother James M. Lamberton, in his address before the Right Worshipful Grand Lodge of Pennsylvania, at the celebration of the "Sesquicentennial Aniversary of the initiation of Brother George Washington into the Fraternity of Freemasons," held in the Masonic Temple, in the City of Philadelphia on Wednesday, November the fifth, A. D. 1902, states:[64]

"It is well known that during the French Revolution religion was dethroned, and reason installed in the place of Deity. The spreading of such doctrines was by many ascribed to the 'Illuminati,' who were supposed to be Masons. During this period clubs like the Jacobin Clubs in France were formed in this country, and the spread of these doctrines was greatly feared, especially by the clergy, and in 1798 one of them, one G. W. Snyder, of Fredericktown, Maryland, wrote to Washington sending at the same time a book entitled 'Proofs of a Conspiracy,' etc., by John Robison,[65] the conspiracy being 'to overturn all government and all religion'."[66]

This letter, sent to Washington at Mount Vernon covered no less than six pages; following is a verbatim copy of the original now in the Library of Congress.

"To His Excellency George Washington.

"*Sir,*—You will, I hope, not think it a Pre | sumption in a Stranger, whose Name, | perhaps never reached your Ears, to ad | dress himself to you, the Commanding | General of a great Nation. I am a | German, born and liberally educated | in the city of Heydelberg, in the Pa | latinate of the Rhine. I came to this |

Country in 1776, and felt soon after my | arrival, a close
Attachment to the | Liberty for which these confederated | States
then struggled. The same attachment | still remains not glowing,
but burning in | my Breast. At the same Time that I am | exulting
in the Measures adopted by our | Government, I feel myself
elevated in | the Idea of my adopted Country, I am | attached,
both from the Bent of Educa | tion and mature Enquiry and
Search | to the simple Doctrines of Christianity, | which I have
the Honor to teach in | Public; and I do heartily Despise all the |
Cavils of Infidelity. Our present Time | pregnant with the most
shocking Events | and Calamities, threatens Ruin to | our Liberty
and Government. | The most secret Plans are in Agitation; |
Plans calculated to ensnare the Unwary, | to attract the Gay
irreligious, and to | entice even the Well-Disposed to combine in
| the general Machine for overturning all | Government and all
Religion.

"It was some Time since that a Book | fell into my hands,
entitled 'Proofs | of a Conspiracy, &c. by John Robison,' which |
gives a full Account of a Society of Free | Masons, that
distinguishes itself by the | name of 'Illuminati,' whose Plan is to
over | throw all Government and all Religion, even | natural; and
who endeavor to eradicate | every Idea of a Supreme Being, and
distin | guish Man from Beast by his shape only. | A Thought
suggested itself to me, that some | of the Lodges in the United
States might | have caught the Infection, and might co-oper | ate
with the Illuminati or the Jacobin Club | in France. Fauchet is
mentioned by Robinson | as a zealous Member; and who can
doubt | Genet and Adet? Have not these their con | fidants in
this country? They use the same | Expressions, and are generally
Men of no | Religion. Upon serious Reflection I was led | to
think that it might be within your | Power to prevent the horrid
Plan from | corrupting the Brethren of the English Lodges | over
which you preside.

"I send you the 'Proof of a Conspiracy,' &c. | which I doubt not, will give you Satis | faction, and afford you matter for a | Train of ideas, that may operate to our | national Felicity. If, however, you have | already perused the Book, it will not, | I trust, be disagreeable to you that I | have presumed to address you with this | Letter and the Book accompanying it. | It proceeded from the Sincerity of my | Heart, and my ardent Wishes for the | common Good.

"May the Supreme Ruler of all | Things continue You long with us in | these perilous Times: may he endow you | with Strength and Wisdom to save our | Country in the threating Storms and | gathering Clouds of Factions and Com | motions! and after you have completed his | Work, on this terrene Spot, may He | bring you to the full Possession of the | glorious Liberty of the Children of God, | is the hearty and most sincere Wish of

"Your Excellency's | very humble and |
"devoted Servant,
"G. W. Snyder.

"Fredericktown, (Maryland) Aug. 22, 1798.
"His Excellency General George Washington."

Sir,

You will, I hope, not think it. Presumption in a Stranger, whose Name, perhaps never reached your Ears, a address himself to you the Commanding General of a great Nation I am a German, born and liberally educated in the City of Heydelberg in the Palatinate of the Rhine. I came to this Country in 1776, and felt soon after my Arrival a close Attachment to the Liberty for which these confederated States

Facsimile of First Page of Letter from G. W. Snyder to Washington, August 22, 1798.

A Thought suggested itself to me, that some of the Lodges in the United States might have caught the Infection, and might cooperate with the Illuminati or the Jacobins in France. Fauchet is mentioned by Rob[ison] as a zealous Member: and who can doubt Genet and Adet? Have not these their confidants in this Country? They use the same Expressions and are generally Men of [no] Religion. Upon serious Reflection I was [led] to think that it might be within your Power to prevent the horrid Plan from corrupting the Brethren of the English [Lodges] over which you preside.

I send you the Proofs a Conspiracy which, I doubt not, will give you Satis faction and afford you Matter for.

Facsimile of Fourth Page of Letter from G. W. Snyder to Washington, August 22, 1798.

113

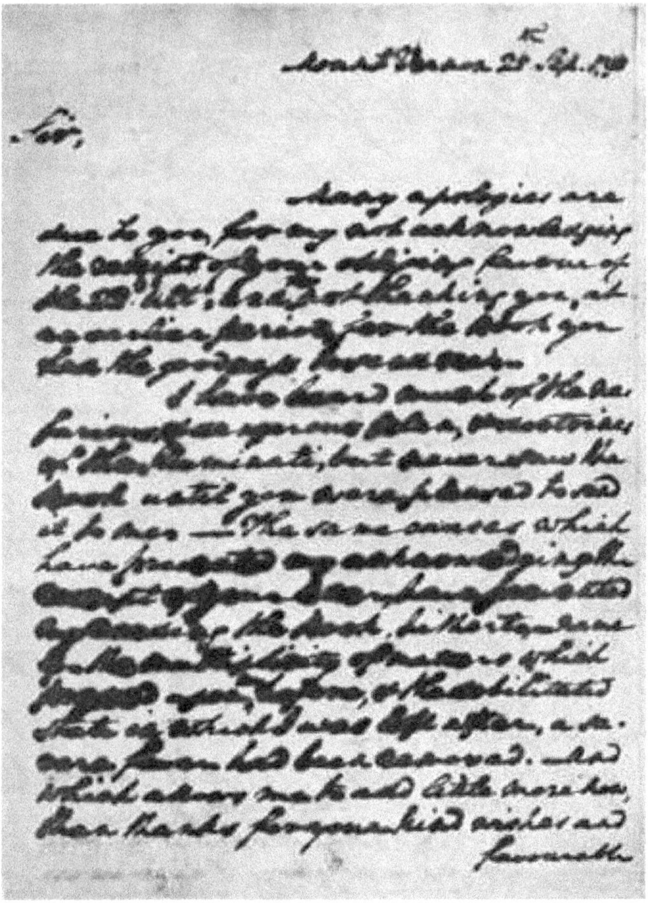

Facsimile of press copy of Washington's answer to rev. G. W. Snyder.—
September 25, 1798.

This man Snyder (Schneider) was an agitator and thoroughly irresponsible person, having no ecclesiastical connection with any organized Church Body.

In the year 1787, Schneider came from Albany, New York, to Frederick, ostensibly to collect money to build a Church. He was kindly received and permitted to preach in the Reformed Congregation, where he soon fomented discord and trouble.

Schneider was soon driven out of Frederick Town, but returned again in 1794, when he renewed the trouble in the

115

Church, which ended in a schism. The matter finally got into the Civil Court, and on February 15, 1800 the case was decided against him, which ended his activity in Frederick Town; soon after which he left for parts unknown.[67]

Snyder, who was not a native of this country, evidently labored under the impression that Washington was a Grand Master General, who presided over all of the English (or Symbolic) Masonic Lodges in the United States. Snyder evidently used the term "English" Lodges, to distinguish them from the Masonic bodies working in the so-called higher (Scotch) degrees, as are now known as the Ancient and Accepted Scottish Rite.

How important Washington considered this correspondence is shown by his precaution in taking a press copy of both of his letters to Snyder, who he was led to believe was the regular pastor of the German Reformed Congregation at Fredericktown. These are now in the Library of Congress. It will be noted that in all of his other Masonic correspondence, copies were made in his regular letter books by his clerks, of both address and reply. Brother Washington evidently surmised that this letter from Snyder was nothing more or less than a scheme to entrap him. It was not until a month had elapsed, and then only after due consideration, that the following reply was sent to Fredericktown, viz.:

"Mount Vernon, 25th Sept. 1798.

"*Sir,*

"Many apologies are
"due to you, for my not acknowledging
"the receipt of your obliging favour of
for
"the 22d ult, and ^ not thanking you, at
"an earlier period for the Book you
"had the goodness to send me.

"I have heard much of the ne-
"farious & dangerous plan, & doctrines
"of the Illuminati, but never saw the
"Book until you were pleased to send
"it to me. The same causes which
"have prevented my acknowledging the
"receipt of your letter, have prevented
"my reading the Book, hitherto, name-
"ly, the multiplicity of matters which
me
"pressed upon before, & the debilitated
"state in which I was left after a se
"vere fever had been removed, and
"which allows me to add little more now,
"than thanks for your kind wishes and
"favourable sentiments, except to cor-
"rect an error you have run into, of my
"presiding over the English Lodges in
"this Country. The fact is, I preside over
"none, nor have I been in one, more than
thirty
"once or twice, within the last years.

"I believe notwithstanding, that
"none of the Lodges in this Country are
"contaminated with the principles as-
"cribed to the society of the Illuminati."

        "With respect
"I am, Sir,
"Your Obed^t H^{ble} Servt

"The Revd Mr Snyder.
Endorsed
to
"The Rev^d Mr. Snyder.
"25th Sep. 1798."

Facsimile of press copy of Washington's second letter to rev. G. W. Snyder.
—October 24, 1798.

In this letter Washington was correct in stating that he had not presided over the "English Lodges in this Country," undoubtedly meaning as Grand Master General.

Where Washington says *"The fact is I preside over none,"* he meant that he did not then preside over any individual lodge, as he at that time was a Past Master of Alexandria Lodge, No. 22, of Virginia.[68]

Where he says *"Nor have I been in one,* [meaning an individual lodge] *more than once or twice within the last thirty years,"* he

119

obviously had in view his occasional visits to the various lodges during that period, and that he could not, on account of his official duties and other conditions, attend any lodge regularly.

As a matter of record, Washington was a member of Alexandria Lodge, No. 39, of Pennsylvania,[69] and attended some of its meetings at Alexandria in 1783 and 1784, as is shown by the Minutes of the Lodge, and the records here presented.[70] Further, that when the Brethren of Alexandria Lodge, No. 39, changed their allegiance from Pennsylvania to Virginia, General Washington was especially named in the warrant, after his consent having been first obtained,[71] and thereby became the Warrant Master of Lodge No. 22, under the Virginia jurisdiction, April 28, 1788, serving as such until December 20 following, when, as the minutes of that date show,[72] he was unanimously elected to succeed himself for the full term, serving in all about twenty months.

The records further show that, in 1778, Washington occupied the chief position in the procession at the celebration of St. John the Evangelist by the Grand Lodge of Pennsylvania at Philadelphia in 1778, in which more than three hundred Brethren joined.[73]

He also occupied the same position when he laid the corner stone of the present capitol at Washington, September 18, 1793, clothed with the Masonic Apron presented by Lafayette, which is now in the Museum of the Grand Lodge of Pennsylvania. Upon both of these occasions, Washington made a public profession of his membership in the Masonic Fraternity.

Records show that Washington was present at the meeting of American Union Lodge (a Military Lodge), at Morristown, N. J., December 27, 1779;[74] at American Union Lodge at Nelson's point on the Hudson June 24, 1782;[75] at King Solomon's Lodge of Poughkeepsie, December 27, 1782, and occasionally at

Alexandria Lodge, No. 39, in 1783-1784, and the Virginia Lodge, No. 22, between the years 1788 and 1797.[76]

Washington in the next paragraph of his letter to Snyder makes his meaning absolutely clear, that while he had not attended any Lodge regularly during the past thirty years he plainly states: "I believe notwithstanding, that none of the Lodges in this Country are contaminated with the principles ascribed to the society of the Illuminati."

This belief is further accentuated by the letter to the Grand Lodge of Maryland a few weeks after the above letter was written to Snyder.

In addition to above records, there are numerous traditions of Washington's occasional visits to Masonic Lodges and functions:[77] all of which fall within the thirty years mentioned in the Snyder Letter.[78]

Further, Washington's great interest in Freemasonry is shown by the many addresses received from different Grand and Subordinate Lodges throughout the Union, all of which he acknowledged in fraternal terms, also by the various Masonic constitutions and sermons dedicated to him, which he received with thanks and were preserved in his library.

It will be noted that in the fifth line from the bottom, "*Within the last thirty years*," which in all Anti-Masonic publications is printed in italics, the word "*thirty*" was not in the body of the letter as originally written, but was an afterthought and interlined before the press copy was taken.

In the press copy of this letter, it will be noted that the word written over the words "*last years*," is almost indecipherable; in the photostat it is completely so. This has led some investigators to question whether the interlined word is really "*thirty*."

The surmise that the blur in the press copy of Washington's letter to Snyder, was "thirty" was first promulgated by Jared Sparks, when he furnished the text of the letter to the Anti-Masonic agitators, during the political excitement which swept over the New England States in the second decade of the nineteenth century.

Snyder, upon receipt of this letter, undoubtedly after consultation with persons who were politically opposed to Washington or antagonistic to the Masonic Fraternity, wrote a second letter and sent it to Mount Vernon under date of October 17, 1798; no copy of this letter has thus far been found among the Washington papers in the Library of Congress.

Washington immediately sent the following sharp reply to Snyder, in which he plainly sets forth his belief that the Masonic Lodges in the United States were not interested in the propagation of the tenets of what was then known as Jacobism or the Illuminati. The words as underscored in the original letter by Washington were to emphasize his meaning upon this subject.

Photostats of both of the above letter press copies are in the Archives of the Grand Lodge of Pennsylvania.

"Mount Vernon 24th Oct. 1798.

"*Rev. Sir,*

"I have you favor of the

tive
"17th instant before me and my only mo:
"to trouble you with the receipt of this let
"ter, is to explain, and correct a mistake
"which I perceive the hurry in which I
"am obliged, often to write letters, have
"led you into.——

"It was not my intention to doubt

"that, the doctrines of the Illuminati, and
"principles of Jacobism had not spread
"in the United States. On the contrary, no
"one is more, fully satisfied of this fact
"that I am.

"The idea I meant to convey, was,
"that I did not believe that the *Lodges*
"of Free Masons in *this* Country had, as
"*Societies,* endeavoured to propagate the
"diabolical tenets of the first, or the per-
"nicious principles of the latter, (if they
"are susceptible of separation) That
"individuals of them may have done it, or
"that the *founder,* or *instrument* employ
"ed to found the Democratic Societies
"in the United States, may have had these
"objects, and actually had a separation
"of the *people* from their *Government*
"in view, is too evident to be questioned.

"My occupations are such, that
"but little leisure is allowed me to read News
"Papers, or Books of any kind. The reading
"of letters and preparing answers, absorb
"much of my time.—

      "With respect,—I remain,
"Revd Sir,
"Your Most Obed^t H^ble Servt

"The Rev^d.
"Mr Snyder."
Endorsed
to
"The Revd Mr Snyder,
"24th Oct. 1798."

It is a historical fact that Washington had always retained the highest respect for the people of Maryland, and especially the citizens of Frederick County. No man ever stood higher in the estimation of the people of Maryland than Washington, and his death awakened genuine sorrow. On February 22d, 1800, memorial services were observed in the Reformed Church at Fredericktown.[79] It was a solemn day and the whole County was in mourning; at which time Ex-Governor Thomas Johnson pronounced the funeral oration. Snyder took no part in these services.

The two letters to Snyder were chiefly relied upon by the Anti-Masons to support their political claims.

"That Washington was never in a Lodge but twice, in his life; that he paid no attention to Masonry during the war; that in 1781 he declined being addressed by Masons as a brother Mason, and in 1798 was very particular to insist upon the fact that he had not been in a Lodge, but once or twice in 30 years, and knew nothing of their principles and practices."[80]

How false these statements so frequently made, is shown by the many proofs here presented in facsimile of the originals, which also absolutely controvert the statement in Governor Ritner's Vindication? viz:—

"That all the letters said to be written by Washington to Lodges are spurious. This is rendered nearly certain: First, by the non-production of the originals: Second, by the absence of copies among the records of his letters: Third, by their want of dates: Fourth, by the fact that his intimate friend and biographer, Chief Justice Marshall,[81] (himself a Mason in his youth,) says that he never heard Washington utter a syllable on the subject, a matter nearly impossible, if Washington had for years been engaged in writing laudatory letters to the Grand Lodges of South Carolina, Pennsylvania, and Massachusetts."[82]

The movement to elect General Washington a Grand Master over all the Brethren in the United States originated at a meeting of American Union Lodge, held at the encampment of the American Army at Morristown, New Jersey, December 15, 1779. This Lodge was a Regimental Lodge of the Connecticut Line, originally warranted by the Provincial Grand Master of Massachusetts.

This movement continued to find favor amongst the craft, especially in Pennsylvania, and culminated in a motion to that effect at a General Grand Communication of the Grand Lodge, December 20, 1779.

This resulted in a Grand Lodge of Emergency being convened January 13, 1780, when the following action was taken:[83]

"This Lodge being called by Order of the Grand Master, upon the request of Sundry Brethren, and also in pursuance of a Motion made at the last General Communication, to consider the Propriety as well as the necessity of appointing a Grand Master over all the Grand Lodges formed or to be formed in these United States, as the Correspondence which the Rules of Masonry require cannot now be carried on with the Grand Lodge of London, under whose Jurisdiction the Grand Lodges in these States were originally constituted; The Ballot was put upon the Question:

Whether it be for the Benefit of Masonry that 'a Grand Master of Masons thro'out the United States' shall be now nominated on the part of this Grand Lodge; and it was unanimously determined in the affirmative.

"Sundry respectable Brethren being then put in nomination, it was moved that the Ballot be put for them separately, and His Excellency George Washington, Esquire, General and Commander-in-chief of the Armies of the United States being first in nomination, he was ballotted for accordingly as Grand Master, and Elected by the unanimous vote of the whole Lodge.

"Ordered, That the minutes of this Election and appointment be transmitted to the different Grand Lodges in the United States, and their Concurrence therein be requested, in Order that application be made to his Excellency in due form, praying that he will do the Brethren and Craft the honor of accepting their appointment. A Committee was appointed to expedite the Business."

The movement was further advanced at a Convention of representatives of the Army Lodges, held at Morristown, N. J., on February 7, 1780, when, fortified by the pronounced action of the Grand Lodge of Pennsylvania, a committee was chosen of which Brother Mordecai Gist of Maryland was chairman and Brother Otho Williams of Delaware, secretary.[84]

Facsimile of Final Letter from Boston, Ending the Attempt to make Gen. Washington General Grand Master.

This Committee issued the celebrated address:

"To the RIGHT WORSHIPFUL, The Grand Masters of the several Lodges in the Respective United States of America.

"UNION——FORCE——LOVE."

This address was signed by representatives of no less than seven states, viz.: Maryland, Connecticut, New Jersey, Pennsylvania, Massachusetts Bay, New York and Delaware; in addition to those of the American Union Lodge, Artillery, St. John's Regimental Lodge and the Staff of the American Army.

It was further ordered that the foregoing address with an exact copy of these proceedings signed by the President and Secretary, be sent to the respective Provincial Grand Masters in the United States.[85]

It was not until the middle of October that a reply was received from the Grand Lodge of Massachusetts to the circular letter sent out by the Grand Lodge of Pennsylvania, and then only in response to a letter written by our Grand Secretary, Rev. Brother Dr. William Smith.

This matter led to more or less correspondence between the Grand Lodges of Pennsylvania and Massachusetts and was in abeyance, until January, 1781, when the following letter was received from Joseph Webb, Grand Master of Massachusetts.[86]

"Boston, Jany 17, 1781.

"Rev*d* Sir and
"Respected Brother

"Last Friday Evening the Grand Lodge met, agreeable to adjournment and after a long debate on the subject, whether it was expedient at present to elect a Grand Master General for the United States, it passed in the negative.

"Inclosed I transmit you the vote from the G. Sec'y.

"Yr Affect*e* Brother
"& Hble Serv*t*
"Jos: Webb.
"Rev Dr Smith
"Philadelphia."

The belief that Washington was the Grand Master of the United States was widespread, and, as our late Bro. James M. Lamberton said in his address before mentioned,[87] notwithstanding the fact that the project to elevate General

128

Washington fell through, "that the action of the Army Lodges and of our Grand Lodge got abroad, is shown by translations of two letters from a Lodge at Cape Francois,[88] on the island of San Domingo, directed to General Washington as Grand Master of all America, soliciting a charter, which were presented to our Grand Lodge, February 3, 1786. The same thing is shown by a medal struck in 1797, the obverse showing the bust of Washington, with the legend, "G. Washington President. 1797," the reverse showing many Masonic emblems,[89] with the legend "Amor. Honor. Et Justica G.W.G.G.M." (*i. e.,* George Washington, General Grand Master).

The writer of the letters to Washington, Snyder, quoted at the beginning of this chapter, being of foreign birth, and not a member of the Masonic Fraternity, nor even living where a Masonic Lodge existed, evidently labored under the same delusion as the Brethren at Cape Francois.

The Masonic Correspondence of Washington as represented upon these pages, should settle for all time to come the question, as to the esteem in which Washington held the Masonic Fraternity, of which he was an honored Member.

It is stated that there are still a large number of Washington papers in the Library of Congress, that are not accessible, as they have thus far not been classified or indexed. Thus it is in the possibilities that there may be still further documentary evidence found of Masonic import, in addition to such as are set forth upon these pages.

Footnotes:

[64] "Memorial Volume, Washington Sesqui-centennial Anniversary," Philadelphia, 1902, p. 165.

[65] "PROOFS | of a| CONSPIRACY | against all the | RELIGIONS and GOVERNMENTS | of | EUROPE | carried

on | in the secret meetings | of | FREE MASONS, ILLUMINATI, | and | READING SOCIETIES, | " collected from Good Authorities | by | JOHN ROBISON, A. M. |— EDINBURGH, | 1797. |

[66] The original letter of August 22, 1798, is among the Washington papers in the Library of Congress; a photostat of same is in the Archives of the Grand Lodge of Pennsylvania.

[67] Cf. Historical sketch of the Evangelical Reformed Church of Frederick, Maryland, 1904, pp. 22-25.

[68] Cf. "Washington, The Man and Mason," p. 288.

[69] *Vide* "Sesqui-Centennial Anniversary of the Initiation of Brother George Washington before quoted," p. 149.

[70] Cf. Chapters II and III *supra.*

[71] Cf. "Washington, The Man and Mason," p. 286.

[72] *Ibid.,* December 20, 1789. His excellency, General Washington, unanimously elected Master; Robert McCrea, Senior Warden; William Hunter, Jr., Junior Warden; William Hodgson, Treasurer; Joseph Greenway, Secretary; Dr. Frederick Spambergen, Senior Deacon; George Richards, Junior Deacon. Extract from Minutes, p. 288.

[73] *Vide* "Freemasonry in Pennsylvania, 1727-1907," Vol. I, Chapter X, pp. 295 *et seq.*

[74] *Ibid.,* Vol. I, Chapter XII, pp. 399 *et seq.*

Vide "Washington and his Masonic Compeers," Chapter VIII, pp. 149 *et seq.*

[75] *Ibid.,* pp. 86-87. Also records of King Solomon's Lodge, No. 1, Poughkeepsie, New York.

[76] *Ibid.,* pp. 150 *et seq.*

[77] *Ibid.,* pp. 139 *et seq.*

[78] Washington, so far as known, attended the following public Masonic functions:

1. Procession in Philadelphia, Festival of St. John the Evangelist, December 28, 1778.

2. Festival of St. John the Baptist, June 24, 1779, with the American Union Lodge, at the Robinson House on the Hudson, New York.

3. Festival of St. John the Evangelist, December 27, 1779, with American Union Lodge, at the Morris Hotel, Morristown, New Jersey.

4. Festival of St. John the Evangelist, December 27, 1782, with King Solomon's Lodge, at Poughkeepsie, New York.

5. Festival of St. John the Baptist, June 24, 1784, with Lodge No. 39, at Alexandria, Virginia.

6. The Masonic funeral of Brother William Ramsay, February 12, 1785, at Alexandria.

7. Laying of the cornerstone of the capitol at the Federal City (Washington, D. C.), September 18, 1793, upon which occasion Washington walked in the procession.

[79] Cf. Historical sketch before quoted, p. 24.

[80] Anti-Masonic Republican Convention before quoted, p. 26.

[81] Grand Master of Virginia, 1793-1795.

[82] Vindication of General Washington before quoted, p. 15.

[83] Cf. "Reprint of Minutes of Grand Lodge," Vol. I, p. 19.

[84] "Freemasonry in Pennsylvania, 1727-1781," Vol. I, p. 39.

[85] Address in full, *ibid.*, pp. 399-402.

[86] All of the original correspondence is in the Archives of the Grand Lodge of Pennsylvania, Mss., Vol. A.

[87] "Washington Sesqui-Centennial Celebration, Nov. 5, 1902, Memorial Volume," pp. 135-6.

[88] Cf. "Old Masonic Lodges of Pennsylvania," Vol. II, Chapter LIII, pp. 242-250.

[89] Specimen in Museum of Grand Lodge of Pennsylvania.

www.ingramcontent.com/pod-product-compliance
Lightning Source LLC
Chambersburg PA
CBHW071549040426
42452CB00008B/1120